SO-CRT-719

THE TROUBLE WITH
CHRISTIANS,

The same Bible...
the same God...
the same trouble.
by Zola Levitt

THE TROUBLE WITH
JEWS

© Coypright 1996
Zola Levitt Ministries, Inc.
All rights reserved.

This book is dedicated to Israel,
then, now and always my love.

Table of Contents

The Trouble with Christians

The Trouble with Christians: What to Do

The Trouble with Jews

The Solution

Appendix A: A Christian Example

INTRODUCTION

As I have pursued my ministry over 25 years, I have noticed a tremendous lack of Bible comprehension on the part of Christians, and no Bible study whatsoever among the Jews. Since I was born and educated as a Jew and came to Jesus Christ in 1971, I have lived a relatively full life in both communities. In fact, starting from my first day of Hebrew school, I have spent 25 years being educated and practicing as a Jew, and 25 being educated and practicing as a Messianic Jew (or a Christian, as some would have it). In those 50 years, I noticed quite a few peculiarities in each of those great communities, and I believe it is time I made some observations.

I began this book at the beginning of the 90's in Israel. I distinctly recall starting it while looking out of a hotel room window at the Sea of Galilee. I continued to carry the manuscript and a tape recorder on all of my tours, and to do odd amounts of work here and there at home. I feel qualified to speak about everyday life in the Jewish and the Christian communities, not because I am necessarily a scholar of either one, but because I have lived them full-blown as a practicer. As a Jew I was seven years in Hebrew school, ten years in Sunday School, bar mitzvah and confirmed, and I have fought for Israel all my life in whatever ways I could. As a Christian I have loved the Messiah, Jesus Christ, since March 14,

1971, and served as He directed every day since that time. In the next year after I received Christ, I went into full-time ministry and have not taken a dollar from the world since that time.

As to this book, I can quote the advertisement for it in our ministry catalog to explain what it is about:

> The trouble with Christians and the trouble with Jews is exactly the same: both subscribe to the God of Israel, the Creator God, the God of Scripture, but both have been remiss in actually reading Scripture. The different denominations of Christianity and of Judaism utilize Scripture differently, but it is patently obvious that the vast majority in either camp doesn't have a significant grasp of the Bible.
>
> The polyglot divisions of Christianity and the arguing factions of Judaism can all be traced back to a lack of knowledge of Scripture. Finally, the crucial difference on the Messiah comes down to that same lack of knowledge.

Chapter 1. The Bible

The Bible contains the earliest written definition of Christianity. The term literally means "Christ in one" and is used in Luke's biographical record of the actions of the apostles:

And when he had found him, he brought him unto Antioch. And it came to pass, that a whole year they assembled themselves with the church, and taught much people. And the disciples were called Christians first in Antioch. (Acts 11:26)

Interestingly enough, virtually all of those Christians at the beginning were Jews. To take the scriptural record literally, the Gospel was disclosed at Antioch only to Jewish people:

Now they which were scattered abroad upon the persecution that arose about Stephen travelled as far as Phenice, and Cyprus, and Antioch, preaching the word to none but unto the Jews only. (Acts 11:19)

In those early times, the Gospel seemed relevant only to those who had a background in the Old Testament with its Messianic prophecies and divine definitions of sin and repentance. Indeed, the first (Jewish) Christians who saw a Gentile saved in the Church age (Cornelius in Acts 10) were "astonished" that a Gentile could conceivably believe in a Jewish Messiah.

> *And they of the circumcision which believed were astonished, as many as came with Peter, because that on the Gentiles also was poured out the gift of the Holy Ghost." (Acts 10:45)*

A proof text for Gentile salvation soon follows (Acts 11:18) however, and, in time, the "strangers" took to the Gospel so enthusiastically that the nomenclature "Christian" virtually came to mean "non-Jew."

But those are technicalities. The important point is that "Christians" refers to people indwelt by Christ: saved people, born again people, or however one wishes to say it, they are true believers who trust in Jesus Christ for their salvation. C. I. Scofield draws a good distinction: the "confessing" rather than merely the "professing" church. [1] (The Lord Himself draws distinctions between believing and unbelieving churches in Revelation 2 and 3. While each church is examined critically, the sixth one, Philadelphia, receives only commendation from the Lord: "I know thy works: behold I have set before thee an open door, and no man can shut it" [Rev. 3:8]. The Lord uses this church as an example of the true church

He will eventually remove from the earth before the coming tribulation period of the End Times: "Because thou hast kept the word of my patience, I also will keep thee from the hour of temptation, which shall come upon all the world, to try them that dwell upon the earth" [Rev. 3:10]. In the other churches the Lord finds major faults. To the church at Thyatira, He said: "Notwithstanding I have a few things against thee, because thou sufferest that woman Jezebel, which calleth herself a prophetess, to teach and to seduce my servants to commit fornication, and to eat things sacrificed unto idols." There is even an "in between" church, that of Laodicea, which the Lord regards as lukewarm, ". . . neither cold nor hot, I will spue thee out of my mouth" [Rev. 3:16].)

The trouble with Christians is that they do not really study the Bible, and thus they do not know the genuine principles of Christianity. Those called Christians have widely divergent views of Scripture, and they seldom arrive at those views by their own study. They are much more likely to take some pastor's or teacher's word for what the Scripture says than to read it for themselves, even in the more evangelical churches.

Religious history is replete with this error, and it is certainly not confined to Christianity. I visited the sumptuous Blue Mosque in Istanbul, a completely open and cavernous single room in which the worshipper is made to feel almost like a microbe. The stunning, vaulted ceiling hundreds of feet above looked down upon a floor that was empty except for an ornate throne, a "reader's chair." Access to this splendid and dominating pulpit was by a ladder-like series of rungs obviously reserved solely for the reader. The guide disclosed that from this chair, two or three stories above the heads of the massed congregants, the reader intoned the holy writ (the Koran). The whole picture was that of what the Book of Revelation calls Nicolaitanism, a term which seems to refer to the conquering of the laity or, in modern terms, the domination of the congregation by an all-powerful priesthood. I ascertained from our guide that the folks in the mosque did not have a copy of what the reader chanted, but merely took his word for the will of their god. There was no discussion, no question period. One is reminded of the medieval Roman Catholics who hunted down Bible translators lest ordinary church members lay their hands on an intelligible copy of the Scriptures.

In a practical and murderous modern example, the Koran was interpreted in a shirt-pocket-size booklet given to Egyptian soldiers during the 1973 war against Israel. "Kill the Jews wherever you find them," the pamphlet exhorted, claiming to quote Moslem scripture (and truth to tell, the Koran can be faulted for such excesses). The problem was that those carrying the booklet were barely conversant, as are most of the adherents of Islam, with any conception of Moslem brotherhood, peace or religious obligations, and were merely turned into killers by those purporting to represent some inspired word. [2]

In modern Christianity, with its proliferation of Bibles in a wide choice of translations, there is no reason for congregants to simply take the word of preachers. It is not that a preacher is necessarily mistaken, but simply that he is given a power never anticipated for him.

Apparently, the more compelling the preacher, the more truthful his teachings seem, so that we have a situation in which ordinary men simply invent doctrine, even though there already is an unimpeachable written source:

All scripture is given by inspiration of God, and is profitable for doctrine, for reproof, for correction, for instruction in righteousness." (II Tim. 3:16)

Obviously, without consultation of the original source there would be no reliable way of making any two churches consistent in doctrine. That is almost the situation we find in Christendom today. Not only are there literally thousands of "Christian" denominations, but the churches within any given denomination are, more or less, dissimilar and even in opposition to one another.

The situation is similar to the American court system, or that of any other constitutional government, to the degree that the courts agree on their interpretation of the Constitution (that is *if* the Constitution is ever read). One should be tried by the same standards and receive the same judgment no matter where one is tried within the land. And while that is the theory, in practice seeking a certain venue or a certain judge might lead to a profound change in the verdict. But, at least with the courts, it is finally agreed that the law of the land is the arbitrator. The law may be interpreted liberally or narrowly and argued skillfully or less so by attorneys, but ultimately all citizens agree to be bound by what they regard as the law applicable to everyone and accused or excused by it equally. That it is written down somewhere and may be consulted at will is without question.

In the churches, however, it is not nearly so clear that there is a defining standard which supersedes local preferences or interpretations. Interpretations of the Bible vary among churches, from those who hold it to be the inerrant Word of God down to those who consider it a book of moral lessons and fables, an outdated relic, composed by well-meaning but fallible sages of old. The doctrinal approaches of churches vary from those trying to hold to an exact reproduction of the customs and practices of the first century church (or even of the Old Testament legal system) to those whose doctrine is made for them by national councils or elected "holy men" of international stature or, most often, simply the neighborhood minister.

When we choose a judge, he is nominated and then examined and his interpretations of the Constitution questioned (as with Supreme Court Justice candidates at Senate confirmation hearings), but the election of church overseers, who are assumed to be more in touch with God or "more reverent" than the average churchgoer, is without biblical precedent. In fact, the idea of distinct denominations with their own councils is specifically criticized in Scripture:

> *Now I beseech you, brethren, by the name of our Lord Jesus Christ, that ye all speak the same thing, and that there be no divisions among you; but that ye be perfectly joined together in the same mind and in the same judgment. For it hath been declared unto me of you, my brethren, by them which are of the house of Chloe, that there are contentions among you. Now this I say, that every one of you saith, I am of Paul; and I of Apollos; and I of Cephas; and I of Christ. Is Christ divided? Was Paul crucified for you? or were ye baptized in the name of Paul? (1 Cor. 1:10-13)*

In omitting true verse-by-verse Bible study, the churches not only diverge on doctrine but, finally, on the nature of God Himself, seemingly remanufacturing Jehovah, Jesus and the Holy

Spirit for the needs of the given community. J. B. Phillips' brilliant work, *Your God Is Too Small*, concerns the remarkable number of available Christs to be found among the churches (resident policeman, parental hangover, God-in-a-box, pale Galilean, etc.). In my book, *The Bible: The Whole Story*, the chapter entitled "The Remanufactured Christ" deals with this issue. Obviously, if "Christians" cannot agree even on the nature of Christ, they will hardly agree with each other.

Arguments for the legitimacy or credibility of Scripture are beyond our scope here; there are many volumes available on that subject. But whether or not Scripture is to be taken as "inerrant," "God-breathed" and "inspired," it at least ought to be discussed outside of politically motivated church councils. And if Scripture is found to be the Word of God, then it seems pointless to operate a Christian church without consulting the Bible constantly.

Because of their lack of biblical direction, Christian people have erred on every side. They are viewed as punishingly moralistic or murderously bigoted. They have gone from a "scarlet letter" kind of condemnation (unlike the biblical example of the Lord who never condemned a sinner) to the burning of witches or the "kill a Jew for Christ" battle cry of my father's boyhood in Latvia. Christians, carrying crosses and wearing robes, actually rode through my father's town outside of Riga, the capital, shooting into Jewish households on Good Friday evening to avenge the death of the One who said, "For this (sacrifice) was I born." And Christians, at least Christians in name, have earned those reputations through a variety of excessive behaviors of the past. The murderers of the Crusades and the Inquisition are, of course, guilty of not just confused doctrine, but ultimately of false Christianity. Their church and its priesthood was so divorced from Scripture as to simply represent a bloodthirsty and totally worldly army fighting a politically-motivated war. They lacked the vaguest comprehension of biblical Christianity.

But the misunderstandings implicit in those notorious errors still infect all Christendom today. The hierarchies we create out of mere men, and even out of mere sins, attest to a lack of biblical knowledge. The astounding variety of Christians in the world speaks of the same lack.

Although they fit no biblical definition of Christianity, sacramentalists, Eastern churches, liberal denominations which have no claim to the Gospel, and all variants of claimants in between are essentially thought of as born again believers. We might as well compare the American denominational Protestant, whose every effort is given to having the most likable possible personality, with the Irish terrorist, Protestant or Catholic, given to killing something in whatever name he considers worth killing for. They are both supposed to be following the same Lord, and they have a written testimony of that Lord's behavior.

Odd variations, such as the Amish and Mennonites reaching back a century or so (but no more) in their customs, the ornately costumed Coptics, and Eastern picture worshippers, show the amazing variety purportedly gleaned from a simple Gospel. The plain black suit of the Amish man who strives for separateness from the world is in vivid contrast to the stunning costume of the fully robed Pope or the cardinals of the Roman Catholic church, though they would both cite the same authority as validating their practices.

This is not meant as a personal bias or criticism of any sect; when comparing Scripture with practice they all seem inexplicably and equally in error.

Chapter 2. Doctrine

The average church member has no real idea of what is biblical, as opposed to what is church-made, in matters of doctrine. They may not recognize that simple things like dress and behavior are typically based on cultural, while very critical points like the doctrine of salvation and witnessing to spread the Gospel are biblical. (One could say that behavior or manners of dress are biblical, to some degree, but where Scripture has kept silent about these things the manmade doctrines are overwhelmingly complex and extra-biblical.) But manmade, or church-made, or community-made doctrines usually take precedence over the biblical ones in actual practice. Most churches work by the rules of their founders or their governing councils rather than by the original source of all correct doctrine: the Bible.

The doctrine of salvation is a good example of what men have done with a central biblical concept. Salvation in Christ is explained in Scripture and in no other place. All other commentary on salvation is just that — commentary. But, oddly enough, men have made an entire catalog of salvation requirements, while Scripture itself requires nothing other than faith for salvation. Since it is "the free gift of God" (Eph. 2:8, 9), nothing is done by men to obtain it. There is no behavior, denomination or state of mind that qualifies one for the salvation purchased by Christ. The

biblical formula is "faith plus nothing equals salvation," but in various churches we require, for
example, baptisms done this way or that ("in
Jesus' name," "in the name of the Father, Son
and Holy Spirit," etc.) and second baptisms, as in
"receiving the Holy Spirit." Other works of merit
are also proposed for salvation.

In my book with Dr. Merrill Unger, *God is
Waiting to Meet You*, we stated that salvation is
simply belief in Jesus Christ alone, and we went
on as follows:

> A complete list of God's requirements
> for entering His eternal plan of salvation
> would involve only one item — faith in
> Christ. By faith and faith alone are we
> saved.

> Salvation in all its limitless magnitude
> is secured so far as human responsibility
> is concerned on the *one* condition of be-
> lieving in Christ as Savior. Believing is
> receiving.

> To this one requirement no other ob-
> ligation may be added without violating
> the Gospel of grace. To add any other
> stipulation is "deserting Him who called
> you by the grace of Christ" and taking up
> with "a different gospel which is really
> not another" but a distortion of "the gos-
> pel of Christ" (Gal. 1:6-7).

> To intrude some form of human works
> or merits into the Gospel of salvation is

to do violence to clear scriptural teaching (Jn 3:16; Eph 2:8-9) and to totally disrupt the essential doctrine of salvation by grace alone (Titus 3:4-5), which is the heart of the Gospel (Titus 2:11-14).

By the very nature of the case, salvation is that which can be wrought by God alone, and solely on the principle of sovereign grace. Salvation is a work of God and in no sense an attainment of man. To introduce some form of human works with supposed merit is to attempt to do what only God Himself can do and has done through Christ.

Every feature involved in salvation presents an undertaking which is superhuman. To be accomplished at all, the whole transaction must be performed by God alone. Man must realize that the only relation he can sustain to this great transaction, once setting it in motion by his faith, is to depend on God to work it out in him.

Salvation through faith begins with those mighty transformations that make a Christian what he is. It involves forgiveness of sins: past, present, and future. It guarantees the safekeeping of the believer. It assures him of eventual glorification and full conformity to Christ at the resurrection.

It promises a home in heaven.

"Only Believe"

Faith + nothing = salvation.

It seems so simple, and it is. But the apostle Paul, in his second letter to the church at Corinth, stressed that Satan would blind unbelievers to this simple truth (2 Cor 4:4). He also deceives believers, to sully their full freedom and joy in Christ (Gal 1:6-7).

He has been successful to some measure. The Lord's own people are divided on doctrines, misguided into cults, and stunted in Christian growth by legalism and other errors. And there is vast misunderstanding among believers of the simple procedure for salvation. Some of the church have been guilty of professing an "amplified" Gospel — one that adds other requirements to faith.

Instead of "only believe" — the true Gospel message — we hear "repent and believe," "believe and be baptized," "believe and profess Christ," "believe and crown Christ as Lord," "believe and confess sin," or "believe and implore God to save you," etc.

At best, amplified gospels amount to wrong directions. A person may still get to the destination, but at some inconvenience. At worst, an amplified gospel is a perverted gospel — a denial of the true Gospel, in effect, a false gospel. The apostle invoked a double curse on false gospels because they set aside the true way of salvation and substitute a false way that precludes salvation (Gal 1:6-9). [3]

One manmade doctrine accepted in several denominations is transubstantiation. This teaching holds that the bread and the wine eaten in Communion, or the Lord's Supper, actually become the body and the blood of the Lord. Scriptural sanction for this fantastic concept is lacking; in order to arrive at that conception, one has to deal literally with what is obviously a metaphor. It seems to me that lack of knowledge is at the root of this extraordinary doctrine, specifically lack of knowledge of the significance of Passover.

In my book *The Miracle of Passover*, I explained the Jewish historical background and significance of the bread and wine as given in Scripture and Jewish tradition rather than in some invention of Western doctrine. The book explains the different actions at the table during the Passover Seder. The bread is handled in a very special way:

After the first cup the father takes three loaves of the unleavened bread and places

them in a special white linen envelope
which has three compartments. A "loaf"
of unleavened bread looks like a big soda
cracker, rather than what we now think of
as a loaf. It is flat, marked with stripes
from being grilled and pierced with holes
from the cooking process.

In a special ceremony of his own, father removes the *middle* loaf from its com-
partment, breaks it, wraps it in a separate
piece of white linen and hides it away. He
"buries" it behind the cushion on his chair,
usually, though some fathers prefer to put
it away in a drawer or under the table.
(Father, and sometimes everyone else, is
seated on pillows for the Passover meal.)

Other elements of the service are explained
until we come to the significant Cup of Redemption, which is actually the Communion cup:

Now comes the most beautiful and
touchingly symbolic part of all — the third
cup, which is The Cup of Redemption. It
is now time to bring forth that buried loaf
of unleavened bread . . . [The loaf] is
sometimes recovered by a child. Father
must redeem it in silver . . . That buried
unleavened bread — the middle piece! —
is then eaten with the third cup of wine.
And that is where we get communion . . .

Father pronounces blessings over both the bread and the wine individually and these blessings have great meaning for us. . . . Jesus, as "father" at His own Passover table, also said these blessings, and it should be noted that the Jewish blessings do not change — they have been said the same way for millennia. Look at Matthew 26:26:

And as they were eating, Jesus took bread, *and blessed it*, and broke it, and gave it to the disciples, and said, Take, eat; this is my body.

When demonstrating the Passover in a church, I ask at this point, "What did Jesus say in His blessing over the bread?" . . . Jesus said this, and these were His exact words:

Blessed art Thou, O Lord our God, King of the universe, Who *bringest forth bread from the earth*.

Then He said, This bread is my body.

Get the connection? He was saying, "Brothers, I know you're concerned about me and all the threats that have been made against me. I know you've heard me say, 'The hour is come.' But don't worry. God has been bringing forth bread from the earth since the beginning of creation, and *this* bread, as I've just told you, represents my body. *God will bring my body forth from the earth!*"

Wonderful! Jesus foretold His resurrection in that blessing over the bread! [4]

Obviously, the original significance of the bread and the wine in the Lord's Supper is much more believable than the almost magical conception that the elements turn into His real flesh and blood as they are eaten. The latter version bends toward mystery religion; in simple terms, it is unscriptural hype to intrigue people, made necessary not by a lack of appreciation but by a lack of knowledge of the original meaning.

The very sober nature of Communion in many churches is a way of adding solemnity and pathos to a celebration originally meant to be totally victorious. There is an amazing difference between the Jewish celebration of a 3,500-year-old emancipation and the Christian "funeral" commemorating eternal life for every believer! The very silence and decorum of the Lord's Supper in some churches is a hype in itself which runs contrary to the original meaning of this crucial element of Christian worship.

Another departure from the Scripture is the veneration of saints, which has led to some almost comical situations. I can recall a certain icon in a Greek Orthodox Church which, until plexiglass was invented, had its paint kissed off by the faithful. Then they covered the icon, but got germs from the plexiglass; and finally we saw lar town, like so many other small towns, suffered under the weight of legalism where local pastors cited what they supposed were scriptural laws to bludgeon the people into an obedience system supposedly pleasing to the Lord. I applied the above Scripture and prayed that it would take hold.

The second story has to do with an amazing "legend" that I actually tracked down myself and found, at least according to local testimony, to be true. It seems that in the late nineteenth century a certain confectionery store in Ithaca, New York, was serving ice cream sodas to the after-church crowd, and the worshippers enjoyed the confection immensely. In fact, it appeared that they really only met at the church to get together for the delicious ice cream soda luncheon, at least in the eyes of the church fathers. A meeting of deacons produced the fact that this fellowship was evil because soda water was, they declared, intoxicating. They approached the confectioner with their conclusion and demanded he stop serving the evil stuff on the Sabbath.

The druggist laughed and informed them that soda water was the equivalent of plain water and not at all intoxicating and he would serve it all the same. The church applied pressure on the faithful not to attend, and finally, negotiation produced a compromise. The confectioner withheld the "intoxicating" carbonated water and served only the ice cream and the syrup. He called this concoction a "Sunday."

Now the deacons came by again, pointing out the evil of naming a mere culinary delight after a holy day, and with much negotiation another compromise was reached: the confectioner agreed to spell the name of the confection differently. And so beginning at that little store in Ithaca, New York, we began to use the peculiar American term "sundae" for the delicious confection, a perennial hit any day of the week!

Jesus took the Pharisees to task more than once for their misunderstanding of the Sabbath, for their rules and regulations which were a tremendous burden to the Jewish faithful. He said to them, "The sabbath was made for man, and not man for the sabbath" (Mark 2:27). The Sabbath was meant to be a blessing. Most Christians are aware of the Sabbath's place in the Ten Commandments:

> *Remember the sabbath day, to keep it holy. Six days shalt thou labor, and do all thy work: But the seventh day is the sabbath of the LORD thy God: in it thou shalt not do any work. . . . For in six days the LORD made heaven and earth, the sea, and all that in them is, and rested the seventh day: wherefore the LORD blessed the sabbath day, and hallowed it. (Exodus 20:8-11)*

Why did God rest? Because He was tired?

mandment concerns an inner attitude of the heart:

> *Ye have heard that it was said by them of old time, Thou shalt not kill; and whosoever shall kill shall be in danger of the judgment: But I say unto you, That whosoever is angry with his brother without a cause shall be in danger of the judgment: and whosoever shall say to his brother, Raca, shall be in danger of the council: but whosoever shall say, Thou fool, shall be in danger of hell fire. (v. 21-22)*

When God commanded the Israelis to eradicate the Canaanites, their external act was to kill, but their internal motive was not murder, but rather obedience to the Lord. God never gave them a blanket command to kill whomever disagreed with them. (In contrast, many Moslems have taken the "kill the infidel" passages from the Koran and turned them into excuses for modern "holy" war, particularly against Israel. The sabotage of Pan Am 103 and the bombing of the World Trade Center and all the rest of the terrorism by the Moslems is justified, they say, by holy writ and, indeed, the Koran has been a source of violence against people of all faiths for thirteen centuries.)

God's approach to sin and the sinner is very different from the church's. A good example is the woman taken in adultery, as related in John 8:1-11. The emphasis is on Jesus saying,

"Woman, where are those thine accusers? Hath no man condemned thee?" She replies, "No man, Lord." And then He says, "Neither do I condemn thee." The point of the story is the lack of condemnation, because He has already given the standard for a correct judge of her: one who is without sin, who can cast the first stone. Well, He Himself does qualify, so there is an adequate judge of her under the Law and she should by rights be stoned. And He says, in effect, "Here is my judgment, I do not condemn thee." So she is exonerated even though she is guilty.

The fact is, all sin is forgiven by the sacrifice of Jesus Christ, and that is all there is to that. There is not a single sin, save unbelief (the blasphemy of the Holy Spirit — Mark 3:29) that the Gospel does not forgive. In our discussion on grace we will stress the sheer amount of forgiveness available through salvation in Christ.

While anecdotes could be piled on by the thousands in this touchy and much-discussed area, I can relate one from my own experience which points up the odd predilection with the particular area of sexual sin. I spoke once at a church where the service could not get started on time because of the long line of young girls whose skirt lengths were being measured by a few crusty old deacons out on the porch. Using some standard of sinfulness (probably the lust in their own hearts), they were pinning crepe paper on the hems of skirts of junior high school girls in order to purify the church. And they somehow made it look as if the sin were in the girls and not the deacons. When the church is more concerned with hems than hearts, something is seriously wrong.

Chapter 3. Christology: The Nature of Christ

Obviously, the nature of Christ is all-important to salvation and to living a Christian life. Clearly, God became incarnate to demonstrate a human life well-lived, and if we understand as exactly as possible how Christ lived, we will approximate the Christian life that much better.

There is no authoritative source outside of the Bible itself that describes the nature of Christ. Endless books have been written on the subject, but they are, of course, commentaries on the original. I like to say that you can gather knowledge of Christ from three sources: the Gospel, the Gospel and the Gospel. [6]

Just as clearly, if we do not read the biblical descriptions and teachings about the career of Christ, we will have only a secondhand idea of His nature, character, ministry and teachings, and we will tend to have a different Christ in our minds and hearts than the biblically revealed Christ. In the author's book *The Bible; The Whole Story*, the point is made that modern people tend to "remanufacture" Christ to fit our times and styles. And it follows that no two of us remanufacture Him exactly the same way. Worshipping somewhat different Christs, we come up with somewhat different ideas of Christianity and therein lies a great deal of the trouble with Christians:

> The re-manufactured versions of Christ
> that I myself find objectionable have to

do with our forgivable way of casting just anyone at all into our favorite mold. Jesus has somehow become a Westerner, under American biblical analysis, more or less a capitalist in His dealings and teachings, and somebody who would fit in well with most of our modern-day plans. [7]

Just before Christmas in 1991, *The New York Times* ran a ludicrous front-page story about two "theologians" who have put out books purporting to disclose the true nature of Christ as discovered by scholarship. We have in recent times a new Christ we might call the "thought-provoking Christ," who is of interest to those who worship what they call scholarship, which is just man's wisdom. These thought-provoking "Christs" always run counter to the Gospel, sometimes diametrically. One theologian after many, many years of study decided Jesus did not say some of the things attributed to Him in the Gospels, but He did say other things. The other one supposed He was married. Conclusions reached by these scholars, who sit in distinguished chairs at some of America's most respected universities and seminaries, seem completely ridiculous. There are no sources for such information about Christ and no reason, other than the scholarship game in which they garner respect and funding for proclaiming dramatic trivialities, for their conclusions. But it must be appreciated that *The New*

York Times did not devote an inch of its newspaper before Christmas to the real Christ, neither on the front page nor the back. That is never done by any media other than the occasional truthful Christian media.

Some of the more radical Christs of our time include the Christ who promotes terrorism; the Christ who is the object of almost mystical sacramental ceremonies; the Christ who heals all comers; the Christ who tells people what tie to wear and finds them parking places; the Christ who is impatient and less accessible than His mother, Mary, who is more likely to answer your deepest petitions; and so forth.

It seems that all of these remanufactured Christs are Gentiles. The only Jewish Christ is the biblical one. There are not any false Jewish Christs. In fact, the first thing to be dropped about Christ when He is remanufactured is His Jewish heritage.

We have still less conception of the truly Jewish nature of the Messiah. As I pointed out on page 1 of my book, *Jesus, the Jews' Jew*, a lady found out from her pastor that Jesus really was Jewish and she said, "If that's true I don't see how I can respect Him, even though He's my Savior." We have reinvented Him as an American Jesus — gentle, meek and mild — or maybe that is the British Jesus we imported. This version of Christ never existed in the Gospel. We seem to have copied the behavior of some cosmic Eagle Scout and made that into our Jesus, although the real Jesus bears no resemblance to this interpretation.

When I made the transition from talk-radio to television, I did the two simultaneously for a while. People tended to react to my television program by calling the radio show, and one day a woman complained about my appearance, saying that since I looked so unimpressive, perhaps I would have done better to stay on the radio. My real looks — bald, bearded, small of stature — disappointed her completely. I asked, "You supposed that I was tall and blond?" She replied, "Yes." And I said soothingly, "Like Jesus?" She said, "Yes."

It certainly goes without saying that no one knows the height of Jesus, but His stature and coloring would, of course, be that of a near-pure bred Israeli. (We have His genealogies in the books of Matthew and Luke, and the only Gentiles among two thousand years of Israeli natives are Ruth, Rahab, and possibly Tamar.)

If you do not know Christ, you just are not a Christian. You certainly cannot be indwelt by a remanufactured Christ and then think you are on the right track. Basing some kind of religion on a mythical character is no better than any personality cult, such as that of the Iraqis who try to emulate Saddam Hussein, or the Russians with Lenin, or the Germans with Hitler. Those we copy are not always bad, of course. Many have tried to follow the example of fine people, but have, of course, fallen short of salvation because human beings are not God's example of how we should believe and how we should worship.

The message of Christ is to be interpreted by each person, as is, for instance, the message of Mozart. We certainly would not try to evaluate Mozart without listening to his music, and in the same way, God has provided us with enough direct information about Christ to make up our own minds and to see a similar Christ from person to person. If we do not read that record, of course, it is hopeless. When we do, we might come up with Christs with slightly different emphases, but the Scriptures allow that; there are different gifts and different missions.

But there is only one true Christ.

Chapter 4. Manners and Mores

A key problem with Christianity as it is practiced today is that it is full of pretense; there is a supposition that everybody is good. We are all following some Christian ideal that we understand perfectly, and what slight slipups occur are just the fault of life on earth or our flesh, etc. We are hooked on the "best people in town" syndrome so that we think we honor Christ the most if we are well-liked and conforming (while Christ Himself was neither).

As part of our being the "best people," we choose odd crusades and causes to be involved with. A church in Dallas flew a large number of people to San Francisco to pray there for the sins of that city, as though Dallas had no sins of its own (or prayers are heard only on location). It is supposed that all real Christians will vote the same way. So-and-so may be the "Christian candidate" or the one most likely to appeal to churchgoing folks. The Rev. Jerry Falwell made a great deal out of this with a supposed "Moral Majority" some years ago, but it was not clear whether those people were really a majority (or moral). The "Christian Coalition" was a later version of this same thing.

We follow nutrition and nutritional trends; that seems to be a Christian trait nowadays. I can remember that once electric cars were a Christian project. It is Christian to prospect for oil in Israel. Some of our activities are for pure profit, but are still somehow considered very Christian indeed. The so-called Prosperity Doctrine teaches that giving to God makes good sense, since God will be obliged to return the gift with interest (up to a hundredfold). One preacher, particularly targeting the poor, repeatedly claimed that sacrificing one's last dollar to his ministry would bring personal profit to the giver (or, more accurately, the *investor*). Most Christians do not seem to give to the Lord's work for the sheer joy of that giving. Perhaps without tax deductions there would be far less Christian giving.

Christians appoint odd heroes. Marine Lt. Col. Oliver North, who came to fame only as a defendant in the Iran-Contra hearings and who seems not to claim born again status for himself, was called to Christian broadcasts and to speak in churches. He even ran for U.S. senator on the basis of his wholesomeness and solid values, although the people of his state apparently did not fall for it enough to elect him. One evangelical once told me that the prime example of a Christian was President Ronald Reagan. When I criticized Secretary of State James Baker in my newsletter for his browbeating of Israel, our ministry received letters saying that he, too, was a born again believer, or at least that he "had faith." One letter continued as follows:

> Your choice of words was appalling, but your ignorance of his character should

be an embarrassment for someone in your position whose aim, supposedly, is to influence others in Christian faith. It appears you chose to judge him based on your disapproval of his views rather than find out what sort of man he really is.

Jim Baker is a Christian. In his remarks made at the National Prayer Breakfast, 2-1-90, he spoke of his hesitancy in discussing his personal journey of faith. He said, "But here I am, and I want to talk to you briefly about faith, about friendship and about our collective spiritual responsibilities." He stated further, "Like many of you, I am just one person genuinely struggling to put faith into practice in my life, but over these last nine years in Washington I have gained some valuable insight into that practice."

The missing statement is "I received Christ as my Savior on (date)." Obviously, what some Christians accept as a Christian standard falls below the biblical minimums. As long as an individual conforms to our "best people" model, he is assumed to be a good Christian.

As a church, we esteem certain American-Christian types: the white-haired preacher, the silk-suited evangelist, the shouting crusader against sin, the gracious lady of means and pedigree who gives of her time and substance to the church, etc., etc. Certain "crusades" are sanctioned as being the best endeavors to which good Christians should devote their time and resources. We chase after pornography, we chase after the New Age Movement, we picket the streets about abortion, and we overlook the multitudes of children dying every day in the Third World for want of the simplest concern. Not long ago, Christians came out in nationwide force to picket the strange movie *The Last Temptation of Christ.* Ninety-nine percent of them had not seen it, but like the radical Moslems who demand the death of author Salman Rushdie for insulting their faith, they turned into a resolute mob.

The biblical virtues of caring for widows and orphans, visiting the sick and those in prison, feeding the hungry, clothing the naked, and so forth, get lip service and some action, but nothing at all compared to the righteous indignation displayed by the crusaders. Biblically, the Lord established a standard (at least for those individuals concerned with the prophesied tribulation period) of Christian conduct as follows:

> *For I was an hungered, and ye gave me meat: I was thirsty, and ye gave me drink: I was a stranger, and ye took me in: naked, and ye clothed me: I was sick, and ye visited me: I was in prison, and ye came unto me. . . . And the King shall answer and say unto them, verily I say unto you,*

*inasmuch as ye have done it unto one of
the least of my brethren, ye have done it
unto me. (Matt. 25:35-36,40)*

It should be stressed that these particular standards of judgment fall upon Christians under the enormous pressures of the tribulation period when the Antichrist will rule the world and Christianity, as biblically practiced, will be a capital crime. Many will be martyred for displaying their faith in those scriptural ways mentioned previously. Therefore, how much more easily can we live up to those same standards in an age when Christians are relatively undisturbed, generally well-off, and living, for the most part, in peaceful nations like the United States? Simple logic urges that Christians of good times qualify, at least morally, alongside those of the worst times.

Basically, Christians think they must *act* like Christians, but in doing that they actually act like a Western-Christian ideal and not like Christ or Paul or Peter. If they wanted to act like the original Christians, one would suppose the first thing they would do would be to consult the Scriptures about how the original Christians behaved. They would certainly learn something about Judaism, since all of the first Christians were Jews. In reality, we act like those character types we appoint: the Norths, the Reagans, the Bakers (or, for someone else, Gregory Peck, Tab Hunter, or Charlton Heston; or, for still someone else, Roger Staubach,

Oral Hershiser, or Tom Landry). Expressions used are often those such as, "He's a real brother in the Lord," usually meaning he looks, acts, talks and bears himself like our Western-Christian ideal, not that he is like the Apostles or like Christ. If we appointed an actor to play his part, Tab Hunter might be the archetype. (That goes back a generation, but in reality we do not have this particular archetype today. Heroes of the movies have descended far below any Christ-like standard and are now more often lovable "bad boys" such as Bruce Willis, Clint Eastwood, Jack Nicholson, Don Johnson or Sylvester Stallone.)

The irony is that today's "brother in the Lord" is seldom like Christ or the apostles or Paul at all, because those early Christians had quite abrasive personalities, if the truth be told (or read).

In passing, it might be mentioned that we also will overlook a bona fide, born again believer (or at least someone who claims that for himself and appears to live the life) when we disagree with his policies. President James Carter was an active deacon of his Baptist church and was doing various good works during and after his presidency, but seemed abandoned by Christians during his term. The politics aside, it seemed that Carter was judged on his effectiveness as a government official and not his commitment to Christ. In the end, he seemed to be abandoned by those Christians who voted him in to begin with. Descending from the realm of the White House, we seem to make the same judgments at every level, down to the family. If Junior leaves college to join a Christian commune, his much more conservative churchgoing family may disapprove, even if he testifies that this was the call of the Lord.

In summary, we like Christians who are well-spoken, tall, perhaps handsome, sincere sounding, quite conservative in their values, usually evoking what we consider "old-fashioned virtues." We do not appoint to spiritually high status those Christian individuals who are ethnic (especially Jewish), racially different, of what we consider odd denominations, or those who are less successful at the temporal assignments they are doing. Thus, the suave denominational minister of graying temples and decades of experience in the pulpit is considered the honored Christian, but the street minister who witnesses to the unwanted is not so honored. President Reagan is just next to the Lord; President Carter is not. And so it goes.

None of this, of course, is arrived at with the slightest consideration of the biblical standards or definitions of their works.

Chapter 5. The Church

Our style of going to church is localized, indeed. The Western church bears little resemblance to the New Testament church. We said some of that in the section on doctrine, but here we will deal with the peculiar Sunday worship service that has been adopted by trial and error in the Western world.

It requires mandatory attendance like the Old Testament Temple, but it should be understood that attendance was legally required at the Temple because sacrifices were mandatory to atone for sin. The Temple was God's dwelling place on earth ("And let them make me a sanctuary; that I may dwell among them" [Ex. 25:8]) and sacrifices were effective only at this location. It escapes most Christians that the majority of the Jewish people did not attend the Temple every Sabbath — they had much less formal local synagogues for that — but they were required to go to the Temple at three festival seasons per year: Passover, Pentecost and Tabernacles.

The Western Church has become so set in its ways that when the first missionaries came to Israel, they held their services at 11:00 a.m. on Sunday mornings in English. The Israelis — what few were interested — could not attend at 11:00 a.m. on Sunday because Sunday is a workday in Israel and, besides, they did not speak English. Actually, if God were at His post only at 11:00

a.m. on Sunday in the American time zones (say Virginia Beach, Tulsa, etc.), it would be Sunday evening in Israel.

As to the service itself, we have made a little pageant that we are comfortable with, but that bears no resemblance at all to New Testament worship. We have what we call a minister, or a pastor; but there is no precedent in the Bible for such a person, at least not as we have styled him: teacher, counselor, general C.E.O. of the church with his name on the sign outside. (Nor is there a precedent for the rabbi in the Old Testament.) Our pulpit committees, stewardship and membership committees, and so forth, seem necessitated by our style of worship and the sheer size of our church bodies, but, again, they have no sanction in Scripture. Our seminaries differ in styles and teachings. To celebrate Jesus Christ, who had only one robe, Dallas Theological Seminary students must wear a suit and necktie to class every day. Those at Moody Bible Institute until recently could not wear beards, though undoubtedly the Lord and His disciples did and, in fact, the institute's founder, Rev. Dwight Moody himself, did also.

I myself made those at Moody Bible Institute uncomfortable when I spoke there since I, too, wear a beard, but I was one of Moody Press' best-selling authors and so they grimly sat through my remarks.

By and large, the church today focuses on

"external" qualities in its leaders, rather than measuring their qualifications according to the specifications of the Word. The job a minister does today requires a very different set of gifts from that listed in the New Testament, as can be seen by the following:

Today's Requirements:

fund raiser
dynamic personality
orator
C.E.O.
administrator of staff
chair of committees

New Testament Requirements:

to feed the church (Acts 20:28)
oversee the flock (Acts 20:28)
an example to the believers (I Tim. 4:12)
continue in doctrine (I Tim. 4:16)
labor in the Word (I Tim. 5:17)
able to teach (I Tim. 3:2, II Tim. 2:24)
willing to work at a trade (as Paul did in Acts 18)

The minister of today is considered a fine minister indeed if he is a great orator. A compelling style of speech-making seems to take precedence over knowledge of Scripture. The requirements we have today for a pastor are practically the same as those for any corporate executive. Although these skills can certainly be useful to a minister of God, it is the inner spiritual gifts and the attitude of the heart that are of paramount importance.

Music also important in most churches, as indeed it was in biblical worship. But there is an enormous variety in the approach of individual churches and denominations to the music they use in their services, from decorous congregations using symphonies, to charismatics with a full brass band accompanying a type of spiritual hoedown, to the Church of Christ with no instruments allowed at all. And these are all reading the same New Testament.

The three-hundred-year-old music used in many churches is peculiar. We play no Bach or other serious Christian music, in general, other than ancient hymns which are well below the musical understanding of even the children in the modern audience. The music is very dated and, if the truth is told, sometimes unscriptural. J.B. Phillips, in his book *Your God Is Too Small*, lists some hymn phrases that are misleading, if not outright distorted. Verses such as "Gentle Jesus, meek and mild/ Look upon a little child" and "Christian children all must be/ Mild, obedient, good as He" conjure up a picture of a timid Jesus, someone who might have trouble working up enough anger to whip the money-changers out of the Temple. Others seem to imply that faith is a form of escapism, as in "Hide me, O my Savior, hide/ Till the storm of life be past/ Safe into the haven guide/ O receive my soul at last." And there is almost a sort of holy masochism in "Oh to be nothing, nothing/ Only to lie at His feet/ A broken and emptied vessel/ For the Master's use made meet [fitting]." [8]

Choirs today barely read music in churches where they could be singing the magnificent cantatas of J. S. Bach Sunday after Sunday and learning a new one for each service (at the speedy rate at which the master composed them)! We are more likely now, in the larger churches, to hire professional musicians, unbelievers or whomever, to perform the more difficult pieces like Handel's *Messiah*, which congregations once sang on their own. As a young oboe player, before I came to Christ, I was glad to have Easter or Christmas "gigs" in churches. They paid well, the audience was not overly discriminating, and the music was relatively straightforward and simple. The only difficulty church jobs presented to the musicians of the time was that it was difficult to sneak a cigarette, since there were no intermissions.

The idea of bringing unbelieving musicians to the church brings to mind an unusual but relevant Old Testament prohibition:

> *And as for the perfume which thou shalt make, ye shall not make to yourselves according to the composition thereof: it shall be unto thee holy for the Lord. Whosoever shall make like unto that, to smell*

> *thereto, shall even be cut off from his*
> *people. (Exodus 30:37-38)*

God gave specific instructions for the making of the incense to be used in worship, and issued a dire warning against anyone making a synthetic type, "like unto that" of the real incense. An important prohibition is given concerning worship: No "strange" incense is to be offered. This speaks of simulated or purely formal worship. [9]

What seems to be meant is that the worship wafting up to God ("the perfume") should not be artificially created. Praise to God through music must involve hearts that have been made "holy for the Lord." Bringing in unbelievers to add worldly talent to Christian worship is simply unholy. It is just one more way that the church has gotten off track because Christians do not know the Scripture, which is the foundation of our faith and therefore should be the foundation of our practice.

Chapter 6. Prophecy

It is hard to imagine at this time in the affairs of men a more crucial subject than biblical prophecy. If it is true — if it is even only half true — then absolutely nothing can take precedence over this knowledge. The calamities that are to come upon the earth as forecast by the Bible prophets are a matter of life and death for almost every soul and, in this case, I mean the second death, the permanent one.

Even on a lesser level, prophecies about the geopolitics of the End Times would certainly be helpful to know if there is any truth to them at all. How enlightening it would be, for example, to realize that all prophets agree that Israel's destiny is secure and the Jewish people are not to be removed from their land ever again.

> *And I will bring again the captivity of my people of Israel, and they shall build the waste cities, and inhabit them; and they shall plant vineyards, and drink the wine thereof; they shall also make gardens, and eat the fruit of them. And I will plant them upon their land, and they shall no more be pulled up out of their land which I have given them, saith the Lord thy God. (Amos 9:14-15)*

In that case, such matters as peace conferences, border disputes, boycotts and the like might be greatly influenced by a clear understanding of prophecy.

Likewise, prophecies about a coming horrific period of wars and "nation rising against nation," and "famines, and pestilences, and earthquakes" (Matt. 24:7), would surely be a word to the wise about how to make their plans.

Of course, we presuppose that it would be believers who are reading the prophecies, or at least people who would give credence to the works of the ancient seers. Whatever one's spiritual persuasion, people conversant with Scripture are aware that the prophets, at least, have a very good batting average; they have been accurate on a great many things in the view of even casual Bible readers. (The prophets have always been 100 percent accurate, of course, but even allowing room for doubt about predictions in our future, thinking people realize that the Bible is a reliable source of information.)

Archaeologists in Israel rely on biblically described sites to conduct their digs (with good results) and farmers plant their crops where the Scripture reports them as having prospered in ancient days. The dietary laws of the Bible have been examined and found reasonable and beneficial, and the historicity of Scripture — the locations of ancient cities, tribal names, battles, reigns of kings, etc. — invariably proves accurate. Imagined errors of fact or contradictions in Scripture tend to evaporate quickly upon scrutiny of the original.

With all of that said, the Bible is a valuable source of information for people living today. The New Testament says as much of the Old:

Now all these things happened unto them for ensamples: and they are written for our admonition, upon whom the ends of the world are come. (1 Cor. 10:11)

It also recommends scriptural study for the guidance of everyday lives:

All scripture is given by inspiration of God, and is profitable for doctrine, for reproof, for correction, for instruction in righteousness. (2 Tim. 3:16)

But Scripture says nothing more critical than its double message about events to come: believers will prosper and go on to a new kingdom on the earth; unbelievers will suffer the wrath of God according to Scripture and, once the new kingdom begins, be separated from Him forever. Even those totally skeptical of this message should read it. As to the church being ignorant of it, nothing is more inexplicable. In fact, one might say that the church is ignoring its own marching orders. It is surely the responsibility of believers to sound the warning about what is to befall the world, and

if the messenger does not consult the message he
surely can't be very effective. If we don't sound
the alarm, who will?

But the fact is, some churches are the last in
their communities to appreciate that world events
are following a course plainly prophesied in Scripture; and, to get to the bottom line, they really
have never been taught and do not really believe
in their heart of hearts that there *is* a next life.
Christianity is taught as a moral system for rightly
and effectively living this life, and it is that, but
the teaching seems to end there. We end up thinking our faith is all about the here and now and
"what we see is what we get."

If the churches understood prophecy, they
would be a tremendous force in many countries
to inform or influence secular governments. In
the United States a vast majority of citizens at
least respect the idea of church attendance, even
if they do not actually do it, and they form a siz-
able proportion of "watchmen on the wall" (II
Sam. 18:24), in scriptural language. If the leg-
endary Humpty Dumpty, who also sat on a wall,
had received some forewarning of his great fall,
conceivably all the king's horses and all the king's
men might have been able to put him — and their
nation — back together again. At the very least,
they would have been prepared for it.

But truly, this is a serious point. Prophecy
cannot be headed off — "it is written," as the Lord
would say — but at least the church could publi-

cize it and establish its reliability, and that, in turn, could cause many to come to Christ and avoid the coming consequences. (Or they could come to Christ after some, but not all, of the consequences have transpired — such as at least coming to belief during the tribulation period and thus going on to the Kingdom and Eternity with the rest of the believers.) The church would surely do that if the church itself understood the meaning of the hour.

In my own experience, I became a sought-after speaker on prophecy when I had written a single book about the subject and had the least, the most modest, possible knowledge of it. Whole churches were spellbound by a man who had been in the Lord less than one year talking about rather elementary material gathered for one writing project. Still, I was requested in church after church because, evidently, none of those audiences had heard any of my information, which was on the possibilities of the rebuilding of the Temple in Jerusalem (from my book with Dr. Thomas McCall, *Satan in the Sanctuary*). As it is now, I still travel from church to church explaining material that could be mastered over a weekend with a competent teacher and some attention on the part of believers.

The level of questions asked when I speak shows misunderstanding of the most basic biblical principles, which, in turn, shows a real lack of teaching. Prophecy is simply a subject that is hardly touched on in many churches and yet, in order of importance spiritually, it must be second only to testifying of the Lord Himself.

Where the synagogues are concerned, the lack is even more tragic since they have had the oracles of God from time immemorial and all End Times prophecy is applicable especially to Israel and the Jewish people. I will speak of that in the upcoming section, "The Trouble with Jews."

It is difficult for me to leave this discussion of prophecy without presenting at least some basic material on End Times events for the edification of any reader who does not understand this crucial subject. From my book *Once Through the New Testament* (written with Dr. Thomas McCall), I offer the following as the most basic discussion of the highlights of End Times prophecy:

> There are actually three major phases to the return of Jesus Christ that we should discuss separately: The Rapture, the Second Coming, and the Eternal State.
>
> We touched on the Rapture in our earlier discussion about the new message of the church. In essence, the Rapture is a future event in which the Lord will terminate the church age and take all the believers out of the world. The unbelievers will remain on earth to confront the Tribulation Period, and finally God's final judgment.

For the Lord himself shall descend from heaven with a shout, with the voice of the archangel, and with the trump of God: and the dead in Christ shall rise first:

Then we which are alive and remain shall be caught up together with them in the clouds, to meet the Lord in the air: and so shall we ever be with the Lord. (1 Thess. 4:16-17)

Christ will not return to the earth, per se, but will appear in the heavens and call His own with a shout and the blast of a trumpet. The souls of those who have died in Christ through the centuries of the church age will be reunited with the remains of their dead bodies, and the bodies will be resurrected into the same kind of eternal body Jesus had when He rose from the dead. Those who are still alive will also be changed completely, taking on immortal bodies and ascending with the resurrected ones to the Lord's presence (1 Corinthians 15:51-57). All of this will take place "in the twinkling of an eye" and once the Lord has assembled His body, His glorified bride, He will take her across the light years to His heaven.

Two important events await us in heaven after we are united with Christ.

We mentioned the Judgment Seat in the chapter on Revelation; there our ministries on earth will be evaluated to determine the sorts of rewards each of us earned. This is God's incentive program, as it were, and the Judgment Seat will reward the endurance of the saints, the persecutions, the troubles, the sacrifices and all of the good works done in our bodies (2 Corinthians 5:10). Many will rejoice over the gold, silver, and precious stones we have sent ahead, but many will have to reckon with the wood, hay, and stubble accumulated in their lives (1 Corinthians 3:11-15). The Maker of human nature knows how human beings operate. We will tend to be more faithful in His service if there are rewards awaiting us at the end of our service.

The Marriage Supper of the Lamb, the next event in heaven, will be a magnificent celebration where the Church is presented formally to Christ. The Father will perform this indescribably beautiful ceremony (Revelation 19:7-10) and all the saints of all ages will rejoice at this ultimate wedding.

Back on earth the Antichrist will have risen to power in the aftermath of the Russian invasion of Israel. He will claim to be God and undertake his persecution of Israel and those who are preaching the Gospel. The unregenerate world will suffer the Tribulation Period while the church enjoys its most glorious seven years to that point.

The Tribulation, as we have seen, will culminate in the war of Armageddon in which the whole world is involved. The Lord will interrupt this hellish battle with His actual Second Coming to the earth. In the first coming He was the Lamb, sent to be sacrificed. In the Second Coming He is the Lion, sent to rule the world.

He will preserve Israel from certain destruction, judge the nations, and establish His kingdom on earth.

Many Christians dispute the literal kingdom and Christ's personal reign over the whole world. They consider the idea to be carnal and to contradict the teachings of Christ on His kingdom being spiritual and "not of this world" (John 18:36). But here unfulfilled prophecy makes the matter more than clear. There are innumerable prophecies concerning an earthly kingdom that must yet be fulfilled. Jesus taught that the meek will "inherit the earth" (Matthew 5:5) and that the disciples will rule over the twelve tribes of Israel (Matthew 19:28). He confirmed that the kingdom would be restored to Israel, from where He will reign, but He did not reveal the time of the event (Acts 1:6-7).

Furthermore, the Old Testament speaks of Israel being the head of the nations (Deuteronomy 28:13), of all nations flowing into Jerusalem to learn from the Lord (Isaiah 2:1-3), of the knowledge of God covering the earth as the waters cover the ocean (Isaiah 11:9), of nations learning war no more (Isaiah 2:4), and of the wolf and the lamb lying down in peace together (Isaiah 11:6). How will all these prophecies be fulfilled unless Christ returns to the earth and transforms it?

Finally, the length of time of this earthly Kingdom is given in the last book of the Bible. None of the Old Testament or other New Testament books say how long the Messianic reign will last, but in Revelation 20:4-6 we are told several times that it will last a thousand years. Many kings have dreamed of their empires lasting for a thousand years, but only Christ will actually accomplish it.

The third and final phase of the Lord's return has to do with what theologians call the Eternal State. Just as the Church Age is not forever, neither is the Millennium. As good as the Kingdom Age will be, it is not the best, and the best is yet to come.

The last act of all "time" will be God's

judgment of all unrighteous souls. All who have not believed from all ages, from all nations, will be resurrected. They will not be disembodied spirits but will face the Lord in their complete humanity — body, soul, and spirit.

During their lifetime they preferred not to believe, but to rely on themselves and their works. This they will have to do at Christ's Great White Throne. All of their works will be presented in unvarnished truth, and those works in which they trusted will condemn them. All who elected not to be in the Book of Life will be condemned. They will not have the blood of the Lamb to cover their sins and forgive their works. They will be consigned to eternal hell, which is described as the Lake of Fire and Second Death. It is terribly sad, and no one can or should rejoice over the eternal ruination of the lost. They will be separated from God forever; the judgment is final and beyond recall. Once this awful work is finished, the Lord and His people can turn to the most joyous of all tasks, the establishment of the Eternal Order.

Up to this point the only thing the Lord has made that is physically new since the sixth day of creation is the resurrection body. But the resurrection bodies of Christ and His saints must have a suitable place for such resplendent spiritual and physical beings. So the Lord will create a whole new habitation — the New Heaven, the New Earth, and the New Jerusalem.

Words failed John as he tried to describe the visions of the eternal bliss he saw, and he struggled mightily to do so with divine inspiration. The New Jerusalem, our ultimate home, is of special interest. It will be about 1,500 miles on each side, a square at the base about one-half the size of the United States (Revelation 21:16). It will also be 1,500 miles high, which suggests either a cube or a pyramid in shape. The foundations and gates are designed to ensure that we will forever remember the names of the Twelve Apostles and the Twelve Tribes of Israel (Revelation 21:12-14).

Apart from glorifying the Lord we are not told what we will be doing in the New Jerusalem, but we know that our capacity for work, knowledge, and enjoyment will be infinitely greater than it is now.

Much of the above is impossible for the unbeliever to appreciate and difficult even for some believers. It is mystical and we have no experience with such goings-on. The only reason we know it will all happen is because God has said so in

His infallible Word. We walk by faith, not by sight, just as Abraham did when he wandered in tents looking for a city whose builder and maker is God (Hebrews 11:10).

It is surely not unreasonable to believe the Bible even in its most arcane images. The Book has been tested since its inception and human history has answered precisely to its prophecy and reportage. Personalities and events have come and gone exactly as predicted in the past. It would be unreasonable to disbelieve that the prophecies found in the same book will not be fulfilled to the letter in the future.

The climactic chain of events will begin with the Rapture, and so we continue looking upward for that glorious appearance of our Savior Jesus Christ (Titus 2:13). We see more readily now why the aged John, after having written much of the information above in his startling Revelation of Jesus Christ, could only pray, "Come, Lord Jesus." [10]

The Trouble with Christians: What to Do

We will review the previous six chapters again, but this time with a view to applying some reasonable correction of the faults we have diagnosed.

Chapter 1. The Bible

Obviously we will get nowhere in trying to make some kind of unified Christian church if there is not some understood principle of what it takes to be a genuine Christian. The mixture we now have in the churches (the liberals, sacramentalists, fundamentalists, cultics, etc., etc.) is a hopeless hodgepodge that literally cannot be communicated with from any single pulpit. Furthermore, by sound biblical definition it is comparable to the empire of Constantine: it is full of unbelievers made "Christians" by the act of some higher committee, not by acceptance of Jesus Christ for salvation.

I went into a Methodist church and found not a single Christian, and the people I was speaking to were called the Evangelism Committee. I had prepared a message on prophecy, but I put those notes away and taught the Four Spiritual Laws of Campus Crusade instead in an attempt to make someone in that church a believer. It seemed that what was called the Evangelism Committee was really a membership committee involved with getting people to join the church and thus increasing the offerings and building an even finer physical plant. (This church already had a chapel with marble floors and a million-dollar organ. I argued with a church member that the place was overdone in view of it being a house of worship to celebrate a Lord who had no place to lay His head. His answer was, "He does now.")

A copy of the testimony of John Wesley was available in the church and I read it, finding that Wesley was already an important preacher when he finally made the step of receiving Jesus Christ for his salvation. He had apparently already been traveling city to city receiving accolades and addressing large audiences before becoming a Christian at all. I shared that testimony and did the best I could to evangelize the Evangelism Committee.

But I was never asked back. That church remains in my mind and heart as the most empty vessel I have seen in terms of losing its first love. ("I know thy works, and tribulation, and poverty, [but thou art rich] and I know the blasphemy of them which say they are Jews, and are not, but are the synagogue of Satan." [Rev. 2:9]) It was totally lukewarm and the Lord would have spit it out (Rev. 3:16). Its candlestick had long been removed. ("Remember therefore from whence thou art fallen, and repent, and do the first works; or else I will come unto thee quickly, and will remove thy candlestick out of his place, except thou repent" [Rev. 2:15].) (The author's booklet *Seven Churches — Does Yours Fit In?* discusses in full the churches described in Revelation 2 and 3.)

It is important that those in the church understand what a Christian really is, so I would like to share here the story of John Wesley's testimony. Wesley was raised in a very religious household, receiving Bible instruction from a very young age. When he was in his early twenties, Wesley took holy orders and became a minister. He devoted himself to religious endeavors, and yet still he did not grasp the meaning of salvation in Christ. He wrote in his journal that at this time in his life "I began to aim at, and pray for, inward holiness. So that now, 'doing so much, and living so good a life,' I doubted not but I was a good Christian." The concept of grace did not seem to form a part of his definition of Christianity, since he wrote that "by my continued endeavor to keep His whole law, inward and outward, to the utmost of my power, I was persuaded that I should be accepted by Him, and that I was even then in a state of salvation."

By human standards, at this point Wesley was a very righteous man: "I diligently strove against all sin. I omitted no sort of self-denial which I thought lawful: I carefully used, both in public and in private, all the means of grace at all opportunities. I omitted no occasion of doing good: I for that reason suffered evil." And yet, "I could not find that all this gave me any comfort, or any assurance of acceptance with God."

Wesley was trying to earn salvation by good works. Even though he was an active minister, he did not know Christ as his Savior: "I continued preaching, and following after, and trusting in, that righteousness whereby no flesh can be justified. . . . Being ignorant of the righteousness of Christ, which, by a living faith in Him, bringeth salvation 'to every one that believeth,' I sought to establish my own righteousness; and so labored in the fire all my days. . . . I was still 'under the law,' not 'under grace.' "

This changed when God brought into his life a man who "affirmed of true faith in Christ." The idea was new to Wesley, but after he examined Scripture and talked to people who had this faith, he "resolved to seek it unto the end, 1. By absolutely renouncing all dependence, in whole or in part, upon my own works or righteousness; on which I had really grounded my hope of salvation, though I knew it not, from my youth up. 2. By adding to the constant use of all the other means of grace, continual prayer for this very thing, justifying, saving faith, a full reliance on the blood of Christ shed for *me*; a trust in Him, as *my* Christ, as *my* sole justification, sanctification, and redemption." And on May 24, 1738, Wesley "did trust in Christ, Christ alone for salvation: And an assurance was given me, that he had taken away *my* sins, even *mine*, and saved *me* from the law of sin and death." [11]

Salvation doctrine itself is in no way complex. It is a major theme of the Gospel that the most ordinary people were able to take advantage of the offer of the Lord to salvation because it was childishly simple: those converted were to "become as little children," preached Jesus Christ (Matt. 18:3). While the Bible is often accused of being complex, obscure and the like, it takes a really impatient or indifferent soul to imagine that it is in any way difficult to be saved.

When I first encountered the Lord, it was through people in Campus Crusade for Christ showing me their little booklet, *The Four Spiritual Laws*. The whole process took about three weeks, since they requested that I read the New Testament — at least the Gospel of John — and, dragging my feet, I finally did that. But when I am asked to give my testimony, I try to stress what a commonplace and ordinary story it really is because salvation itself should be commonplace and ordinary.

As to those four spiritual laws, they are accurate, all in all, and a wonderful tool for demonstrating a method of salvation in the shortest possible space. (Actually, one could do it with three of the laws below, omitting the first one, which most people take for granted, in any case.)

1. God loves you and offers a wonderful plan for your life.
2. Man is sinful and separated from God. Thus he cannot know and experience God's love and plan for his life.

3. Jesus Christ is God's only provision
    for man's sin. Through Him you can
    know and experience God's love and
    plan for your life.
4. We must individually receive Jesus
    Christ as Savior and Lord; then we can
    know and experience God's love and
    plan for our lives.

The Lord put it succinctly Himself in a discussion with the tricky and recalcitrant Samaritan woman in John 4:10:

> *Jesus answered and said unto her, If thou
> knewest the gift of God, and who it is that
> saith to thee, Give me to drink; thou
> wouldest have asked of him, and he would
> have given thee living water.*

The Lord is more brief even than Campus
Crusade. He essentially tells the woman, "If you
knew who it is that gives salvation, you would
ask for it and He would give it to you." Any person — you, for example, or me — needs only to
understand that much. Of course, as we stressed
earlier, knowing who the Lord is may involve
picking through some misinformation or consulting that singular book about Him, the New Testament, but asking is a very small and simple matter. The thief on the cross, a confirmed sinner
being executed for his crimes, said only this to

Jesus Christ:

> *Remember me when thou comest into thy*
> *kingdom. (Luke 23:42)*
> And Jesus replied this way:

> *Verily I say unto thee, today shalt thou be*
> *with me in paradise. (Luke 23:43)*

The Lord's stress was always on the fact that He had not come to turn anyone away and, indeed, "whosoever believeth in him should not perish, but have eternal life" (John 13:15). In fact,

> *For God so loved the world, that he gave*
> *his only begotten Son, that whosoever*
> *believeth in him should not perish, but*
> *have everlasting life. (John 3:16)*

The above Scripture, often seen on signs held up at televised sport events, gives what is probably the most important act of creation in a nutshell.

It is not the purpose of this section to outline all Scripture that concerns salvation, but no Christian should miss an opportunity to testify. The salvation prayer in the little *Four Spiritual Laws* booklet is perfectly adequate (as is the plea of the thief on the cross):

Lord Jesus, I need You. Thank You for

dying on the cross for my sins. I open the door of my life and receive You as my Savior and Lord. Thank You for forgiving my sins and giving me eternal life. Take control of the throne of my life. Make me the kind of person You want me to be.

Have You Heard of the Four Spiritual Laws? What would happen if on some given Sunday this simple doctrine of salvation were taught in every single church? Probably a great number of people who might have imagined they were saved already would actually be saved, like John Wesley. But they would be glad to make this small extra step of faith in the Lord, and that is the only requirement for salvation.

> *Believe on the Lord Jesus Christ, and thou shalt be saved. (Acts 16:31)*

But there would be a contrary reaction as well, in all probability. There are people in the church who are placed there not by the Lord, but by His enemy. It is their business to operate the church in a manner that obscures salvation doctrine.

The world is just becoming aware of certain Dead Sea Scrolls that were suppressed for forty years (revealed only in 1991) that clearly support the historicity of Christ. Scroll fragments, using Messiah-related terms such as "branch of David" and "root of Jesse" and descriptive phrases from Isaiah 53, refer to a Messianic leader who was put to death by wounds or piercing. The scrolls reflect tenets of Messianic Judaism that have until now been unique to the followers of Christ. "Theologians," seemingly bent on hiding this information, all but threw away these crucial documents that might have saved thousands, or even millions. It should be very clearly understood that there are individuals everywhere bent on a mission to thwart the doctrine of salvation and simply prevent people from becoming true Christians. [12]

There are priests of high calling, and titled ministers, elders, deacons, pastors, etc., who, consciously or unconsciously, inevitably oppose the biblical doctrine of salvation and lead flocks not toward, but away from, the kingdom, if the Scripture is to be believed. No one will ever be saved by hearing a sermon on the good life, or the marvelous moral precepts of Jesus, or the superiority of the Christian way over some other ways of living, or by attending a marvelous church, or by giving large donations, or by singing inspiring hymns, or by wearing fine clothes to worship in, participating in drives to right social wrongs, doing the actual good works of the Gospel (feeding the hungry, clothing the poor, etc.) but not for love of Christ, telling the truth, paying all the government's taxes, and on and on. All of the above, while arguably humanistic and enriching to anyone living today, when done outside of belief in Christ will lead not to heaven but to the opposite destination.

No one was ever saved by being good, no one was ever saved by acting spiritual, and no one was ever saved by anything other than asking the Lord for His free gift, if Scripture is to be believed. Naturally, everything I say here is not the doctrine of my church, nor even what I believe; it is simply what the Bible says, nothing more, nothing less. Nothing is clearer in Scripture than how one is saved. Consider Acts 16:31: ". . . believe on the Lord Jesus Christ, and thou shalt be saved. . . ." None of those good works mentioned above involve that simple requirement that even the smallest children can master completely.

With the above having been said, I can only recommend that those steps be followed. There just will be no consistent Christian church if everyone is believing in a different way, in a different Christ, taught by different denominations, in different lands, and so forth. We could say, more simply, that if we consulted the Bible on this subject we would solve the problem completely. [13] And that will be true of each of the various subjects we have taken up in illustrating the trouble with Christians (and in the next section, "The Trouble with Jews").

Chapter 2. Doctrine

Perhaps all church doctrine would be simplified if we would teach the subject of grace. The church as a whole is unclear on sin and forgiveness and thus invents all manner of doctrines to cover this lack. The following section taken from my book *The Bible; The Whole Story* gives a biblical discussion of the subject:

"I Will Remember Their Sin No More"

Grace is absolute forgiveness. It is the sort of forgiveness not found under heaven but dispensed exclusively by God Himself. It is irrevocable, unavoidable and all pervasive. It operates always. It never fails.

Believers in the Messiah can no more avoid this Grace as they walk through the world than they can avoid being wet as they swim through the sea. Their sins are totally and utterly forgiven and forgotten. All the sins of all the believers are forgiven and forgotten. We are not merely tolerated by God, nor excused, nor found not guilty — we are never even tried. Our sins are "remembered no more" (Jer. 31:34; Heb. 8:12).

There can be no price on such forgiveness, and as a matter of fact, there isn't.

It's perfectly free. Grace is given away freely by God because none of us would be able to pay for it. Having Grace is having a gift certificate. When we have a gift certificate we take it to the store and they give us the merchandise. We owe nothing. It's not that the merchandise is free but that someone has previously paid for it.

The merchandise we receive is salvation, of course, and the pre-payer, the Giver, was the true Messiah. We who are believers in the true Messiah, simply come with our "certificates" — our sincere faith in Him — and the salvation is given to us. Our part of the bargain is the faith and that's all. We have no other works to do, no other human effort, no other accomplishment, no other assignment. We cannot earn Grace nor win it as a prize, and the Lord, according to the Gospels, has ever delighted in giving it out where it is least expected, or perhaps even warranted, in our own thinking.

The main trouble we seem to have with Grace is not believing it will really work. We know who we are, after all, and how bad we are, and we suppose we do not deserve Grace. Oddly enough, though, in that philosophy we don't share God's opinion of ourselves.

How To Get It; How To Use It

This forgiveness — this amazing Grace — is obviously the prime issue in our relationship with God. With it is salvation and eternity and without it is eternal separation from God. Salvation itself depends on this state of Grace.

And so, what's our part in it? What must we do to get it?

Once in a while there's a verse or two right together in the Scriptures which say it all (actually they all say it "all" but we find some easier to comprehend than others). Concerning the interrelationship of Grace, faith, works and salvation, Paul wrote succinctly to the Ephesians:

For by grace are ye saved through faith; and that not of yourselves: it is the gift of God: Not of works, lest any man should boast. (Ephesians 2:8-9)

Sermons by the ream have been preached on those important thoughts above, but evidently the point hasn't been entirely made for the majority of those sincerely seeking a right relationship to God. For again, as with the re-manufactured Christs, some people are knocking at the wrong door. The majority of those called Christians today are seeking salvation through works and not by faith. Even having read the clear ideas in the Scriptures above, they still believe on a gut level that God will respond to what they <u>do</u> more readily than to what they believe. Or perhaps it is because what they do is manifest while what they believe is sometimes shaky and uncertain.

The Scriptures are more than clear, however. Our part is faith, God's part is Grace, and works have nothing to do with salvation.

It is obvious that the grace of God would be superfluous if we could be pronounced righteous by what we do. Since we have looked at the Abrahamic Covenant and the Law, we can see the contrast of God's free promise with the external performances demanded by the Law. Where the agreement with Abraham is concerned, Paul quoted it for the Galatians, who were trying to amalgamate works of legal merit and faith together in order to doubly please God (Gal. 3:2-3). Paul deals with the matter by pointing out that the inheritance from Abraham precedes and supersedes the Law. It is a higher thing: a direct promise of God:

For if the inheritance be of the law, it is

no more of promise: but God gave it to Abraham by promise. (Gal. 3:18)

And he concludes . . .

And if ye be Christ's, then are ye Abraham's seed, and heirs according to the promise. (Gal. 3:29)

Christ would not even have had to come and die if men could have reached a true state of goodness under the Law. If the Law could save us then the Messiah wouldn't have had to come to save us. In simple words:

Is the law then against the promises of God? God forbid: for if there had been a law given which could have given life, verily righteousness should have been by the law. (Gal. 3:21)

Those practicing works for salvation are, in a way, performing the Law over again. They are repeating a past covenant unlike the New Covenant under which we now live (Jer. 31:31, 32). They are a throwback to a simpler (or perhaps more difficult) day when men worked out their salvation, one godly act at a time, with much consciousness of their shortcomings, endless confession and affliction of their souls, sacrifices and all the rest. Huge denominations of Western God-seekers practice voluminous religions of works in order to reach the God who said, "The truth will make you free" [John 8:32]. The Jewish people may have an excuse in rejecting the New Testament, and therefore, at least, offering some logic for taking themselves back to the Law (although with the lack of Temple worship and the sacrifices, the Law is beyond recognition as originally prescribed). The Roman Catholics, the Mormons, most of the Protestant denominations, and all of the smaller cults practice works very vigorously for salvation, frankly admitting to "working out" their positions with God. Probably in all of the rest of the denominations there is still a certain amount of the Galatian problem, since hard work and self-mortification is so tempting and reasonable a human position before God. Surely our Master is pleased by our efforts. Surely our bent backs and sweating brows impress Him to appreciate our sincerity.

The only way to escape such utterly earthbound thinking would be to read the Bible and see what God's plan is, rather than working on what we think it ought to be.

Law And Grace

Since we looked earlier at the Law, we might clarify the subject of Grace by contrasting the two. They mark clearly the difference between the Old Testament and the New. (In fact, it is perhaps the lacking knowledge of the Old Testament in the Church that makes salvation under Grace so elusive an idea. Grace just cannot be realized without some appreciation of what Law is. Churches that particularly emphasize repeated study of the epistles alone, reducing faith in Christ to forms of behavior, very often teach a mixture of Law and Grace rather than pure Grace.)

The clearest distinction between Law and Grace comes in the matter of righteousness. Under the Law God demands it of men and under Grace He simply gives it to them. Under the Law we would have to perform to realize the love of God, but under grace we have it instantly and always, "not by works of righteousness which we have done" (Titus 3:5).

As we saw in our discussion about the Law, it is associated with Moses and with works. The Hebrews in the wilderness personify the awful comings and goings of life under the rule of Mt. Sinai. Grace, on the other hand, is associated with Christ and with faith and love. The enlightened Christian walk is graceful; it has no accusations and no penalties, and it is, without a single exception, successful in the end.

There are no laws in the New Testament.

Law, interestingly, is of greatest interest to the righteous and the blessed. Grace properly seeks out the sinful, whom it saves. Law is for good people, in effect, who are capable of performing good acts and have a way of being obedient to God. Grace is for the bad people, who without it would have no other hope of seeing God. It becomes clear as we study the Bible that there really are very few "good people" even among the venerated personalities of Scripture. Observation of contemporary life turns up some evil too. The conclusion is inescapable, in human experience as in the Scriptures, that Grace, not more and harsher law, must be the way of real salvation. If in fact "All sin and fall short of the glory of God" (Rom. 3:23), then Grace is absolutely necessary. God gives it to us because if He doesn't, we won't be seeing Him and He won't be seeing us. The Law, in the final analysis, is too difficult for even the best of men to obey, and Grace just has to be there. If there were no New Testament, and therefore no Grace, the most sincere and religious of men would have no assurance of ever getting to God, and this is the state of those who read the Old Testament only. Without Grace there is not only no salvation, there is not even a concept of salvation. It not only doesn't happen but people don't even imagine what it is.

Grace began with the cross and the resurrection. The Law did have to be satisfied: it is God's Law, after all. The death of the Messiah — His blood — utterly satisfied the Law in the manner that the blood sprinkled on the mercy seat in the Holy of Holies of the Tabernacle justified men's sins. The Law could be broken, of course, and was broken all the time, but blood was provided as the justifier, and hence the sacrifices. Now Christ, the final sacrifice where there is no sin can rationally serve as a propitiation for every one of us. We are sinners but we are justified by the blood of someone who was not a sinner (Rom. 3:23-25). "Therefore we conclude that a man is justified by faith without the deeds of the law" (Rom. 3:28).

The "Age of Grace" lasts until the Church is raptured and taken to heaven.

Then, in the Great Tribulation, the world will be in anarchy. Following the Tribulation we will have the 1,000-year reign of the Lord, which will be a period not of Grace but of Law again. It surprises some believers to perceive that the Kingdom is a period under Law but it certainly is — and even stricter law than the Old Testament period. Examples are given throughout the Sermon on the Mount of the difficult laws of the Kingdom: "If thine eye offend thee. . . ." The elegant and saving solution to sending a disobedient and rebellious group, such as the Christian church, into so stringent a Kingdom is that "we shall all be changed" (I Cor. 15:51-52). Once in our resurrection state we will find Kingdom Law agreeable and always fair (in the very presence of the King, of course). The unbeliever will find the Law crushing in the Kingdom, and the pressure on him to obtain salvation by turning his allegiance to the King will be effective in almost every case.

At any rate, Grace exists between the cross and the Rapture and is really unnecessary at any other point in God's spiritual economy.

During this Age of Grace, the judgment as to whether or not a person is saved has little to do with his good works. Good works may be a fruit of salvation or merely the better nature of some human being coming out, but the true test under Grace is acceptance or rejection of Jesus Christ. It is odd to suppose that lesser men will go to heaven while those who accomplished more and better works on earth may not, in the end. Some of the "weeping and gnashing of teeth" may be well justified from a human point of view. But God's terms are clear. Under the Law it was works, but under Grace it is the relationship to Christ. If I have five good works in my lifetime and my neighbor has 5,000, it is nevertheless my faith in Christ which saves me, and if he hasn't got that he is lost.

Is it right? Is it fair? We can't evaluate it because it is God's. It is, in effect, "given." But then, we must remember the terms of Grace. That too is "given" to anyone any time, no charge, for eternity!

In contrasting the Law and Grace, a final point might be the effect on the believers' ongoing walk with God. The Law certainly affected people's lives. It caused them to behave principally up to their highest potential, if they were sincere at all about it. Or perhaps it defeated them. But in any case, it had a most profound effect on the works and on the consciences

of those who lived under its potent influence. Grace likewise, affects us in our
walk in this age. Service to the Lord,
rather than performance of duties, is the
theme of our walk, and the Grace which
originally saved us, stays with us to en-
able us to do our good works and services.
We all draw greater strength than we really know about from that constant, reliable, and totally energizing "God loves
me" feeling. We know it to be true just as
we knew it when we were saved, and it
rejuvenates us and arms us for what we
must do before we are changed. We can
well imagine that the effects of the Law
were double-edged; people walked away
from the Day of Atonement in triumph
when the priest had at last emerged from
his momentous interview with Almighty
God. But on other days they walked in
dread, with heavy debts to God unpaid.
The little white lie of yesterday, or the tax
cheating of the day before or the adultery
of the day before that, were afflicting the
soul from the moment they happened and
there was still the sacrifices to be made,
the suffocating remorse to be felt, the un-
bearable weight of the guilt, and the terri-
fying thought that the whole system might
break down under the weight of the sins.
How blessed is Grace under which, prop-

erly taught, we have no such rumblings in our walk with God and no such dread of our Father Who loves us so freely.

Grace may be God's most unappreciated idea. It is invariably taken for granted, mistaken for some sort of "by-law," if not real law in the first place, inadequate for our neighbor's sins, or just a way of God buying us off until He can get us alone up there. It surprises some people that even in the Judgment Seat of Christ in heaven when all believers will go before our King (II Cor. 5:10), our sins do not even come up for discussion. Our works are evaluated as to whether they are of gold, silver or precious stones, or wood, hay and stubble (I Cor. 3:11-15). But our sins are nowhere mentioned. God said He would remember them no more, and as a matter of fact, He seems to have forgotten them. In reality, they were all paid for at the cross, and if we have accepted that cross we simply have no sins. We come to court only to find that we're uncharged. Our <u>works</u> will get us greater or fewer rewards in the upcoming Kingdom, but our <u>sins</u>, about which we trouble so much in our earthly walk, are simple not on the books anymore.

It would be an interesting question, but if all Christians were convinced on the

same morning that their every sin was forgiven and that no penalty awaited their
sins — would they begin to sin more or
sin less? It's a true doctrinal position that
our sins are forgiven, and completely forgotten. We just never seem to act that way.

In any case, that is the contrast of
Grace and Law. The key verse is John's
simple observation, "For the law was
given by Moses, but grace and truth came
by Jesus Christ" (John 1:17). There is no
Law where there is Grace. There is no
accusation nor penalty where there is no
Law.

There is no fault where there is perfect Grace. There is a perfect group of
people in which each one is the best of all
possible examples of himself. It may not
look that way among the people themselves as they study each other, but it certainly looks that way to God. I refer now
to the Church, where Grace manifests itself, and where the believers properly do
their good works in the name of their first
love. [14]

The above teaching is, of course, one man's
reading of Scripture and certain points within it
may be arguable. However, it has been in print
and distributed in thousands of copies for something on the order of fifteen years. I wrote it dur-

ing a time I had good physical reasons to believe my service for the Lord was over (due to grave heart trouble leading to a bypass operation), and I meant all of it from the bottom of my heart. In the time it has been available and widely read, no one has given it much debate. The average letter of commentary on the above writing runs along the lines of the West Texas Baptist preacher who said it was the best thing he had read on the subject in some forty years of preaching and he wished the whole church could hear it. While some detractors may not have written in, I will abide by his wishes and submit it here as perhaps helpful to the whole idea of doctrine.

If we could but agree on a "gracious" reading of the New Testament, I think a lot of confusion over the bits and pieces of Christian behavior might be solved.

At any rate, agreement on the fact that since Christ died, sin is forgiven, would be a good start.

Chapter 3. Christology

Here, of course, the solution is to teach about the Messiah *as He is presented in the Gospel* and there alone. We have one book about Christ, the New Testament, and the views of four Gospel writers on His speeches, acts, crucifixion and resurrection, and that is the end of that. It is, of course, a mistake in logic as well as truth to issue new information about Christ from extra-biblical sources, if we are only reading commentaries on commentaries. In other words, odd theories about the nature of the Man taken from some psychology of His speeches, or some odd writings rejected by the early Church, or some liberal theologian's imaginings, or some purely anti-Christian opinion, will lead us down blind alleys.

A first suggestion would be to teach about His Jewish roots. Probably about three-quarters of the people who term themselves "Christians" would be hazy on the idea that Jesus was actually a Jew, a full-blooded Israeli. His genealogies reaching back for two thousand years are given in the Gospels of Matthew and Luke. It is not a matter of Jewish pride: to disconnect the Messiah from the Old Testament is theological anathema. The New Testament flows naturally from the Old, since the Messiah fulfills the prophecies of ancient times. Furthermore, the nationality of the Man is germane to understanding His teachings. One obvious example of this is the relationship between Passover and the Christian practice of Communion, as we discussed in chapter two of the previous section. Without knowledge of this important Jewish feast, much of the significance of the Last Supper is lost. The Lord was celebrating the Passover meal, on the night before His crucifixion, when He introduced this important Christian observance. His words and actions have a particular relevance to this ritual meal, and demonstrate His fulfillment of this Jewish festival (which was a prophetic "shadow," as described in Colossians 2:16-17) and His identification as the Passover Lamb whose blood covers our sin.

We discussed the "remanufactured" Christs at length in the first section. Naturally, if we do not know what He was really like, if we are only believing in a remanufactured Christ, there is no true connection between us and the real Christ. If Christ becomes a statue, a picture, an ideal Westernized character of politeness and good manners, a great moral teacher, a dispenser of favors, a benevolent policeman (or an angry policeman), etc., we belittle the Gospel and it is unclear how we are saved. The true biblical Christ has become hidden under layer upon layer of remanufactured, imagined Christs. The church has about as unclear an idea of the true biblical Messiah as the first-century Jews had at the first coming of Christ.

It is not that the church does not teach about

the Messiah; of course, that is done most every Sunday in most every church. The problem is in not teaching about the biblical Messiah. Those Christs who have evolved from two millennia of remanufacture are not in the Gospel, and it is hard to comprehend how salvation can result from relating to one of those.

To know the real Christ, the Bible is our only source.

Chapter 4. Manners and Mores

Here we have a problem. People will adopt various manners and mores according to their cultures, their times, their peers, their psychology, and in answer to a hundred other promptings. It is well beyond the scope of this book to discuss all the behaviors of all the churches. Suffice it to say that somewhere between libertine living (because we have freedom in Christ) and antiquated costumes and ways (to show how we deplore the world) is the true path. If the church becomes encrusted with religious ritual, it simply repeats the sin of the temples in the Old Testament. An angry Jehovah was repulsed by the cynicism and hypocrisy in the Old Testament temples, saying, "I have spread out my hands all the day unto a rebellious people. . . . A people that provoketh me to anger continually to my face. . . . These are a smoke in my nose, a fire that burneth all the day" (Isaiah 65:2-3, 5). To look at a corrupt priesthood in, say, the time of King Josiah (II Kings 22:16-17) and see that it was necessary to cleanse the nation of its pagan manners and mores, is to realize that we are prey to this error in any generation.

But to achieve precisely what Scripture admonishes is tricky. If the original says only to avoid excessive adornment and we end up almost laughably conservative in appearance before the world, are we doing well? If Scripture says to witness, did the medieval Church do well to mount such efforts as the Crusades and the Inquisition to ferret out the unbelievers and force their conversions (if that was even the idea of such murderous exercises)? And, all in all, if Scripture tells us to "be perfect," are we to gun down the sinners all around us whom we decide are imperfect? The answer here, as in the above sections, is simply more Bible teaching. What does Scripture really say? Will we, like hundreds of millions of Moslems, follow blindly a manmade tradition (say, veils on women) when the holy writ does not demand it? If Scripture says, "call no man father" (Matt. 23:9), can we correctly refer to a spiritual leader by exactly that term? The worldly religions have much to teach biblical people about the exactitude of their manners and mores in regard to written Scripture, but is that teaching accurate?

The point is obvious: we have to teach the Bible.

Chapter 5. The Church

Here again, the answer is a closer reading of Scripture. The New Testament is replete with discussions of the Church in its universal and local forms. Everyday problems of everyday churches are given throughout the epistles and in the first three chapters of Revelation for our use.

The New Testament admonishes Christians to assemble themselves together (Heb. 10:24-25). And that implies that Christians are to meet, to fellowship, to talk about Christian things and to live the faith together. It seems a great distance from the stagy pageants held in some churches today. These are less a way of living than a kind of show about Christianity, it seems.

A rather interesting experiment is found in some churches today that have smaller home groups within the church that meet together in fellowship. Those church members have evidently discovered that the large church assembly does not conform very well to the requirements of Scripture. For example, it is very difficult to fellowship with hundreds of people on any personal level. The smaller groups seem to allow more of the assembling together asked for in the New Testament. Furthermore, the idea of smaller divisions allows for a greater exercise of the different gifts which are liberally distributed throughout the church. There are gifted teachers, singers and leaders of all sorts who could never get to the pulpit or even the rostrum in the fellowship hall in the average church, but who can function effectively in smaller groups.

Also, a closer reading of Scripture is required to understand the various failings of the early Church. The principles discussed in the chapters on the seven churches of Asia (Rev. 2 & 3) reveal some obvious faults (". . . thou hast left thy first love" [Rev. 2:4]) and some that are more subtle (". . . to eat things sacrificed unto idols. . . ." [Rev. 2:14]). Obviously an in-depth study on the modern equivalents of those principles would be more biblical than simply choosing fine orators whose polished homilies from the pulpit give us very spiritual feelings indeed.

And perhaps it would not be too much to ask to allow the church to be open all the time, or at least most of the time, as, say, the public library is. Individual worship is almost unknown in Christianity, or at least it is in those churches with rather formal worship services. We have fallen lockstep into a situation of worshipping one time a week, which is not at all what Scripture advises. To be closer to what Scripture advocates, anyone would be welcome to approach the Lord at any time and people ought to be at the church as often as they can possibly make it. A Russian immigrant, a very strong Christian, related on my television program that his habit was to pray at all times and to assemble himself together with Christians several days a week. He ended up unfortunately holed up in the American Embassy in Moscow for five years as one of the famous Siberian Seven. When I asked him how he passed those years in that uncomfortable underground chamber, he happily replied, "The same way: in fellowship and prayer." Surely we who have churches on almost every street corner could at least open the doors, so that those who understand the scriptural advice that one day is like another in terms of approaching the Lord can enter them.

The way of reform of the church is the same as with all of the subjects above — we need more biblical study and more accurate application of Scripture to our daily lives.

Chapter 6. Prophecy

This is a subject which is meaningless without the Bible. If we do not read the Bible, we do not understand the slightest principle of prophecy, and that is all there is to that. The Bible is the only book that forecasts the future with any accuracy and we ignore those predictions at our own peril.

Enough was said in the original discussion in our first section to show the importance of prophecy knowledge in the church. It is surprising then that most prophecy teaching is done by imported specialists rather than the regular Sunday speaker. In most of the Christian denominations, no prophecy is taught whatsoever, since most of those denominations make little reference to the Bible on any subject. Where the Bible is read, and taught, there will be discussion about prophecy and the converse is also true. Prophecy knowledge follows biblical study, and a lack of biblical study promotes a total omission of prophecy knowledge.

I will not rehash again how critical this information is to this generation, but suffice it to say here, as we have in the sections above, that more Bible knowledge is the only solution.

Chapter 1. The Bible

For Jewish people not to be at least conversant with the Bible must be one of the most curious facts of all history. This world's best-seller is a Jewish book, written and published primarily in Israel (although some books were written in exile or in transit). Every single writer is Jewish.[15] The poetry, philosophy and certainly the laws are indigenously Jewish (Romans 3:1-2), other than for the New Testament letters from Jewish apostles to the churches of the Roman Empire. The whole Bible chronicles the adventures of the Jews, and them almost alone. The Old Testament and the New Testament are far and away Israel's most important export to the world. It is curious that the Jewish people have so little interest in this remarkable Jewish production.

Furthermore, even if a Jew is unspiritual and not interested in the Bible as Scripture, it is surely worthwhile as a definitive history of his people. The Jews are far and away the oldest people on earth in the sense of never having changed their religion or culture in any basic way for some 4,000 years, since Abraham. Archaeological evidence backs up the historicity of that long story, and there is little question that to be a Jew today is not essentially different than to be a Jew 1,000, 2,000, or 3,000 years ago; something no other people can begin to say. Yet the average Jewish person cannot even estimate the age of Judaism and has little comprehension of the majestic biblical story of this singular people.

And even more essential, the Bible contains the magnificent Jewish law, the only international law still in force today. Rome, in its time, dictated its laws to the world it controlled, which was considerable. But Rome broke its teeth on Israel, and its entire empire and all of its body of laws became virtually extinct. The Jewish law, however, persisted in every Jewish home and in every Jewish heart. Modern Orthodox Jewish people are keeping a law issued thirty-five hundred years ago on a mountain in the Sinai desert, and that certainly makes them unique upon the earth. Even today, if I talked with a rabbi in New York, Johannesburg, Beijing, or at the South Pole (if one could be found there), he would consult the same law and render the same judgment that would be given in any other place. To put the Bible away is to put away that law and that would be tantamount to the British putting away the Magna Carta or we Americans our Constitution.

The Bible is the book that establishes monotheism, outstandingly the view of divinity of the entire world today. Only primitive cultures have more than one God in the twentieth-century world, and there is good reason to credit the Jewish Scriptures with the monotheism of Islam and other eastern religions. (The travels of Jewish merchant seamen to the East and so forth seem to have introduced Bible events such as the flood story into cultures as far away as China and Japan, although empirical evidence is lacking for this theory. King Solomon's fleets covered vast amounts of territory and may well be responsible for the appearance of Chinese Jews, Ethiopian Jews, and other farflung Israelites who are returning to the Land today as we watch.) Monotheism, however, though not easily arrived at, pervades global culture.

Scripture contains prophecy and that is essential. Fully one third of the Bible is prophetic. Whether it is appreciated by the Jewish people or not, prophecy continues to be fulfilled, and as far as the biblical "End Times" are concerned, all of the events — disastrous, happy, or otherwise — deeply involve Israel: the Tribulation, the Antichrist, Armageddon and the Second Coming of the Messiah (or "the coming," as Jewish people would have it) would be incomprehensible without Scripture. The descriptions of the kingdom of God to come, looked forward to by Christians and some Jewish worshippers alike, would be an utter mystery without the Old Testament descriptions and the New Testament directions for how to qualify.

In today's problematical world, cataclysmic enmity against Israel is foreseen as a major theme of the End Times in both the Old Testament and the New. Ezekiel details a huge invasion of Israel by countries from "the uttermost north"

(Ezek. 38, 39), and Zechariah deals with the siege of Jerusalem at the end of the age (Zech. 12, 14). In the New Testament, Jesus Himself gives a clear and objective picture of the very world we seem to have today, including the increase in famines, pestilence and earthquakes (Matt. 24:7), the wars and rumors of wars, and even the odd fact that tiny Israel will be "hated of all nations" (v. 9).

These things are of utmost concern to the Jews, of course, and they are understood only by Bible-reading Christians!

This is not to say that the Jewish people do not venerate Scripture, or at least the Torah (which contains the Pentateuch, or first five books of Moses). Terrific ceremony is giving to standing when its ark is opened, carrying it about, kissing it, a grand ceremonial reading of the Scripture (without discussion). Bar mitzvah boys upon reaching their thirteenth birthdays invariably read a section of Scripture to show their competence and maturity as Jews. Synagogues also sponsor Sunday schools which tend to present biblical passages for memorizing, as well as the history of the Jews, a great deal of which is arrived at from biblical sources.

With all that said, none of this encompasses Bible study. The author was seven years in Hebrew school and ten years in Sunday school, bar mitzvah and confirmed, and still did no real Bible study until he was taught to do that by Christian people.

Chapter 2. Doctrine

Jewish doctrines are virtually all manmade. There is no conception of salvation, the New Covenant, or prophecy in non-biblical Judaism. Israel itself is not understood as a Promised Land, a true fulfillment of prophecy, but rather as a happy convergence of political events and proper arming and funding.

The doctrines of Judaism are very odd to outside observers, especially people familiar with the Jewish Bible. They emanate more from the ghettos of Europe of the last three or four centuries than from Scripture, and they therefore concern a period little understood by non-Jewish people, and certainly not by Bible readers. The famous black suits and hats, including smoking jackets, silk stockings, heroic fur, yarmulkes, and so on, are strictly of that period and have nothing whatever to do with biblical Judaism. In a sense, they almost have nothing to do with rabbinical Judaism either, but rather are offshoots of certain schools of Jewish thought generally led by what might be thought of as "super-rabbis" (one such example was Rabbi Schneerson, the "Messiah" of Brooklyn). That the Gentile world fails to grasp the significance of the Hasidic Jewish dress is understandable; that the Hasids are venerating a three hundred-year-old culture rather than a three thousand-year-old culture is inexplicable.

Modern Judaism can be broken down into

three main sects: Orthodox, Conservative and Reform. In Israel, the so-called "ultra-Orthodox" have become dictatorial and demand that the rest of the nation follow their particular interpretations of Jewish law. The situation is ironically reminiscent of the Imams of Iran and their domination of a nation in favor of their interpretations of Islam. The Orthodox demand the closure of movie theaters on the Sabbath and even cast rocks at cars driving too close to their neighborhoods, not just on the Sabbath but in the hours before the Sabbath, which they consider semi-holy since folks should be preparing for the Sabbath. Their emphasis on modesty of dress for women and other puritanical modes of behavior makes them difficult to live with for the secular Jews. In Jerusalem, they have a neighborhood of their own, the Mei Shearim, which is closed off from the rest of the city. Mei Shearim literally means "one hundred gates," and indeed the gates are shut and the rest of Jerusalem is considered virtually apostate. An "in group" type of learning goes on among these folks, and a Bible student would not stumble over their doctrines in his scriptural research. One would have to study with the ultra-Orthodox themselves to understand what they are doing and how it pertains to Judaism.

Most obvious to pilgrims to Israel — Jewish, Christian and otherwise — is the pride of the Hasidim, who virtually parade in the streets in an outward show of righteousness, like that observed on several occasions by the Messiah Himself:

Beware of the scribes, which desire to walk in long robes, and love greetings in the markets, and the highest seats in the synagogues, and the chief rooms at feasts; which devour widows' houses, and for a shew make long prayers: the same shall receive greater damnation. (Luke 20:46-47)

Therefore when thou doest thine alms, do not sound a trumpet before thee, as the hypocrites do in the synagogues and in the streets, that they may have glory of men. Verily I say unto you, They have their reward. (Matt. 6:2)

The other two major sects of Judaism, the Conservative and the Reform, have doctrines of their own, which differ diametrically from each other and from the Orthodox. The Conservative try to observe a middle ground between modern life and the European custom. They do not affect the black suits, and so forth, but they tend to keep the feasts in a form and to attend synagogue at least on high feast days. They are a middle-ground group of people who have many arguments against the Orthodox and their dominating ways.

The Reform are hard to distinguish in substance from denominational Protestants, taking pride in how liberal and progressive they can manage to be and how thoroughly assimilated into cultures like the American. They tend toward intellectualism and veneration of modern thinkers rather than former sages or scriptural personalities. Their worship is "by the book," which is to say the Siddur, a kind of book of common prayer, and not by Scripture, with which they are unfamiliar.

The Reform themselves break into smaller groups, of which the most curious may be the Reconstructionists. They want to remake Judaism to agree with modern times so that it is better appreciated by the Gentiles around it. One dialogue which I had with a Reconstructionist had to do with Jewish exclusivity and how dangerous that adherent thought it would eventually be. He said, "My rabbi told us that if they resent us calling ourselves Chosen People out there, well we'll just stop doing it." I argued that the idea of being chosen was not made up in some public relations office, but was scriptural. My antagonist said the Bible amounts to primitive writing for an ancient people.

The above sketches of the branches of Judaism are certainly not meant to be complete, but simply impressions from within the community. It is more important to see the results of such unscriptural movements. Assimilation into Gentile cultures can be so complete as to make Jews unrecognizable among their fellows in some places in the world, and that is how certain ones seem to prefer it. Intermarriage is rampant; one theory that the end of the age is now upon us has to do with the idea that there will be a discrete Jewish people in the End Times, but if we wait too long they will be out of existence. In effect, the prophecies have to beat the tendency to inter-marry the Jewish people out of this world.

The intellectualism of the unscriptural Jewish sectors is a kind of last retreat into idol worship. It is hard to criticize a modern Jew for admiring Martin Buber or other accomplished Jewish thinkers or achievements, but intellectual pursuits do not necessarily lead to scriptural truths. I interviewed one such "worshipper" of things of the mind who was completely immersed in a book on Judaism, Islam and Christianity recommended by the *New York Times*. I looked at some of the text and found it totally inaccurate to the Bible, at least in its ideas on Christianity. I told my interviewee, "Jesus did not criticize the Pharisees in these brutal terms. Why don't we open the New Testament and see exactly what He said?"

> *For I say unto you, That except your righteousness shall exceed the righteousness of the scribes and Pharisees, ye shall in no case enter into the kingdom of heaven. (Matt. 5:20)*

My Jewish partner was offended and made

this statement: "Why should I read the Bible when I can read an expert on what it really says!" Later that day my partner, who was also my houseguest, wanted to know if a certain football game was on television and asked for the listings. And I said, "Let's not look at the listings. Let's call an expert on television to interpret whether the game is on." This same debater in any other field would always look to source material rather than commentary for any fact he considered believing.

The anecdotal cases above are not necessarily representative of all Judaism, of course, but simply occurred in the travels of the author. Jewish individuals like these are fairly common, however. They would be regarded by the ultra-Orthodox as apostates, by the Conservative and Reform as average Jews, and by God, if Scripture is to be taken seriously, as ordinary unbelievers.

Chapter 3. The Messiah

As with so much else in Judaism, the Messiah is another thoroughly Jewish conception of which Jewish people have only the vaguest understanding. There are theories upon theories on the nature of Messiah (due to the lack of Bible knowledge). The major theory has to do with two Messiahs, known as ben Joseph and ben David. The first is the suffering servant, as was Joseph in Egypt when he was imprisoned, and the second is the victorious general and king, as was David. The necessity of two Messiahs to biblically unread Jews, is to satisfy two kinds of prophecies about the Messiah. He is both to suffer and to triumph, and the theory of two comings of one Messiah had not occurred to Jewish thinking. In my travels, I have had something on the order of seven kinds of Messiahs explained to me by Jews who are aware of this important issue in Judaism. Isaiah 53, the suffering servant chapter, has created a dichotomy among Jewish teachers. Some hold that it is Messianic, and from that chapter emanates the suffering servant concept:

> *Surely he hath borne our griefs and carried our sorrows: yet we did esteem him stricken, smitten of God, and afflicted. But he was wounded for our transgressions, he was bruised for our iniquities: the chastisement of our peace was upon him; and*

*with his stripes we are healed. . . . He was
oppressed, and he was afflicted, yet he
opened not his mouth: he is brought as a
lamb to the slaughter, and as a sheep before her shearers is dumb, so he openeth
not his mouth. (Isaiah 53:4-5, 7)*

The triumphant and kingly Messiah is obvious in Isaiah 9:6-7 (the same prophet!):

*For unto us a child is born, unto us a son
is given; and the government shall be
upon his shoulders; and his name shall
be called Wonderful, Counsellor, the
mighty God, the everlasting Father, the
Prince of Peace. Of the increase of his
government and peace there shall be no
end, upon the throne of David, and upon
his kingdom, to order it, and to establish
it with judgment and with justice from
henceforth even for ever. The zeal of the
Lord of hosts will perform this.*

The most unbiblical estimation of the Messiah seems to have been the appointment of the
modern day Lubavicher Rabbi Menachem
Schneerson. This aged and infirm scholar, who
never visited Israel, died in 1994, but some of his
more zealous followers expect his imminent resurrection. He could not, of course, begin to fulfill the most rudimentary requirements of the

Messiah, such as being born in Bethlehem of the tribe of Judah, etc., etc. It is noteworthy that the Lubavichers, who are among the most serious and dedicated Jewish scholars, have made this bizarre selection.

Sadly, history teaches that people not cognizant of the Messianic requirements in Scripture are duped into following false Messiahs (which has been true of both Jews and Christians). Bar Kochba and Sabbatiel are two tragic examples for the reader wishing to pursue this phenomenon.

We have the ever-receding Messiah, we might say, of *Fiddler on the Roof.* In that excellent play and film, an aged rabbi not unlike Schneerson is asked if it would not be a good time for the Messiah to come, in view of the suffering of the people portrayed in the play. Rabbi, we have waited so long, they say. And the rabbi, with total resignation, replies that they will have to wait somewhere else. Meanwhile, start packing.

We have Messiah turned into simply an upcoming age of enlightenment, peace and humanistic understanding, similar to the liberal Protestant conception of the world getting better everyday and Christian people bringing in some sort of kingdom with their good behavior.

A great many Jews simply do not believe in the Messiah at all, and these are the "unobservant," or what biblical Christians would call "liberals" or even "unbelievers." Messiah stories become *bubameise* (granny's tales) to them. They roll their eyes and say "when Messiah comes," in the same tone of voice as "when pigs fly." These are the kind of Jews who believe the children of Israel crossed the Red Sea on reeds, that it was really the "Reed" Sea. Some denominational Protestants also believe this ludicrous story, which is actually harder to believe than the original parting of the waters. These people think Messiah is a symbol of some age to come and that maybe the reestablishment of Israel now is the ushering in of that age.

As for Jesus Christ, unarguably the most influential Jew of all time, they have close to zero knowledge. He is patronized as a radical or a great moral teacher, a revolutionary rabbi, a radical anti-Roman crusader, and a hundred other earthbound labels. Sometimes He is given no historicity at all, although Christian scholarship has advanced to the point at which it is difficult for Jews to say He never lived (as they did when I was brought up).

Synagogues give soothing counter arguments to "answer the evangelists," saying Jesus never claimed to be Messiah ("I and my father are one" [John 10:30] and ". . . he that hath seen me has seen the Father" [John 14:9]). The stories of Jesus and the New Testament in general are studied in Israeli high schools, but with a view to defaming (or defanging) the Scriptures. The two-edged sword is dulled with expressions like, "the story of Jesus walking on the water," or "the sayings attributed to Jesus," or "the poetic Christian mythology," or "the parables adopted from earlier Jewish writings," etc.

A case that spread all the way to the Supreme Court of Israel concerned the historicity of Jesus as a person who at least at one time lived in Galilee. A bookstore called The Galilee Experience sponsored a multimedia program with slides demonstrating the personalities of Galilee through history. They included such luminaries as Isaiah and Deborah and reached into the Christian era with Rabbi Akiba and the Talmud writers of Tiberias in the early A.D. centuries. It also included Jesus Christ, inarguably the most famous Galilean ever to walk the earth. And that raised the ire of the rabbis. They attempted to deny the bookstore its merchandise certificate, saying that it was a Christian mission in disguise and that the multimedia presentation was a show game designed to give credence to Jesus. The store, for its part, indicated that no one chronicling the history of Galilee could omit such a personality, whatever their orientation to Him. In the end, the store prevailed and received its certification. It is significant that Jesus, recognized the world over by unbelieving Gentiles, is so undervalued in His own country by observant Jews. After all, Jesus was also a Galilean rabbi.

When I grew up, I was taught that the words "Jesus" and "Christ" are curse words and we were to spit when we heard them in Hebrew school.

These were radical old-country teachings. My father was an immigrant. He came to America because Christians were riding through town in Riga, Latvia and shooting into Jewish houses to kill a Jew for Christ on Good Friday. There is no question that these were at least self-professing Christians. Sometimes they were led by ministers wearing robes and carrying crosses. Obviously, these sacramental church members were not rightly related to Jesus Christ, who said, "You will know My disciples by their love" (John 13:35). But that was hard to explain to the people hiding under the beds, who finally fled their own cultures and brought a wealth of brains and talent to the United States throughout the twentieth century.

And during World War II we called the Nazis "Christians." Of course, the Nazis called themselves "Christians" and had the legend *Gott mit Uns* ("God with us") on their belt buckles.

To bring this story up to date, the contemporary conception of Jews about Jesus is that He indeed lived and that He was a rabbi, and perhaps a gifted rabbi, but His ideas were too far off the norm and He unintentionally formed a Jewish sect so strange to the mainline that it developed into Christianity. This is not so far from accurate, if one regards that Christianity is indeed the daughter of Judaism or, more exactly, Judaism fulfilled. The concept of a Messianic Jew would be that the religion called Christianity is simply more branches of the Jewish olive tree, ever spreading out and nourishing grafted-in branches and fruits, and in the end, the kingdom to come will be occupied by both Jewish and Gentile believers having joined together. When in Christ, "there is neither Jew nor Greek" (Gal. 3:28).

Chapter 4. Manners and Mores

Frankly, the Jews live in a wonderful community. Having lived in both the Jewish and Christian worlds in my lifetime (about 50% in each), I have to testify that the Jewish community is better. It is warmer, more friendly, more enlightened, more culturally aware, more creative. Having said all that, it is a shame to see it so unspiritual. All of the compliments I might make to Judaism are of worldly things. When all is said and done, I prefer the company of believing Christians with whatever failings they may have, because ultimately the only thing worth talking about is God and His will and His plans for the future, in the view of a believer.

Jews live by "tradition," a concept celebrated in the initial song of *Fiddler on the Roof*. They have lived a certain kind of "Jewishness" for literally thousands of years and whether they are desert nomads as they once were, European black-suited Orthodox as some still are, or advanced nuclear scientists in the modernistic laboratories of the U.S., they do things "in the Jewish way." This Jewish style certainly includes things that would be enviable to all communities. They emphasize education, the dignity of the individual, freedom for all, solid family life, good marriages, etc., etc. The Hasidic community would like to boast of these things and, truth to tell, if they were statistically figured out, it is almost a certainty that the Jews would rank high on the list as having accomplished a wonderful social adjustment, and this while being hounded and persecuted for some two thousand years, flying from country to country, assimilating or hiding in ghettos, and finally trying to defend a pitifully small land from maniacal enemies on every border.

You have to hand it to them, the Jews are doing pretty well.

But there is a false Jewish crowd also. The emphasis on material things, the estimation of Israel as a successful geopolitical entity (rather than an act of God and a Promised Land) and perhaps an unseemly worldly shrewdness, do not agree with the scriptural picture of the holy Jew. There is a tongue-in-cheek forgiveness for Jews caught racketeering, selling junk bonds, or prospering by various shenanigans. These excesses are excused with a shrug, as though the paramount concern was that a Jewish person be financially successful rather than spiritually informed. I candidly feel a discomfort in criticizing any of my Jewish brethren, but to discuss Jewish manners and mores fairly, one must mention some negatives. The Jewish way is not always the best of all ways.

Books like *Chutzpa* (which means audacity or impertinence) by Alan Dershowitz present examples of a kind of Jewish style which is purely materialistic and worldly. This is American Judaism at its most assimilated and its most affected and, unfortunately, its most ungodly. Pride and the intellect of a winner like Dershowitz must surely be leavened by his public defenses of rascals and his obvious "do anything, say anything for the good of my client" approach.

Supposedly, Jewish people vote as some sort of bloc favoring liberal policies and Democrats. This probably does not prove true in every election. In general the Jews, a highly persecuted people, have favored an emphasis on personal freedoms and a less powerful central government. They have also sided with other minorities, most particularly the blacks, in many issues. Ironically, in the age of Louis Farrakhan (leader of the Nation of Islam), the blacks have hardly returned the favor. Those blacks who have embraced the Nation of Islam, or have otherwise become Moslems, seem to become anti-Jewish for no good reason. Jews, of course, were instrumental in the Civil Rights movement and typically could be found on the front lines of the earliest struggles. They still favor all possible liberties for all possible downtrodden groups, in general.

Interestingly enough, those Jews who are unspiritual are celebrated by those blacks who are Bible believers. It is well-known that Negro spirituals usually concern Old Testament stories ("Joshua Fit de Battle of Jericho," "Swing Low Sweet Chariot," "Go Down Moses," etc.). Some blacks, very conscious of their own period of slavery, side with their brothers in bonds, the Old

Testament Jews. Yet other blacks, conscious of their period in slavery, accuse the contemporary Jews, with no evidence in fact, of having been slaveholders in colonial America.

The celebration of worldly accomplishment is replete in the Jewish community, and the truth is that there are many accomplished Jews to celebrate. A terrifically impressive list of actors, musicians, doctors, lawyers, scientists, etc., can be compiled, and often has been. The whole world knows that the Jews excel in the professions, and it sometimes takes exception on that very point. "The Jews own all the banks," goes the old saw, assuming that Jews are crafty and far ahead of the competition and thus control the money and ultimately cause depressions and cataclysms. This nonsense reaches its apex in conspiracy theories which hold that the Jews are taking over the world. (All fifteen million of them versus 5.5 billion Gentiles!) In countries where there practically are no Jews (Japan, for instance), the Jews are cited for causing market fluctuations, poverty, etc. The Jews have been scapegoats from time immemorial, and we can see the same phenomenon in ancient Egypt when they were slaves, and throughout the A.D. centuries in Europe and the Moslem nations. The Jews were supposedly responsible for the bubonic plague, having allegedly poisoned the wells. They were not getting the plague as readily as the Gentiles simply because they were obeying Old Testament laws about washing the hands before eating, keeping the latrine a certain distance from the kitchen, and other sensible Old Testament recommendations. Probably the Jews of the Middle Ages were more in tune with biblical reasoning than the more advanced and worldly Jews of today.

Anti-Semitism has cost certain nations a great deal. A list of just Russian and German Jews who fled Europe during twentieth century pogroms and Nazism would read like a who's who of science, medicine, and the arts. Names like Horowitz, Rubenstein, Irving Berlin in music, and Einstein and others in science, give some idea of the eminence of the Jewish contribution to a host nation. The entertainment industry could be said to be almost dominated by Jewish people in America. PBS has aired a two-hour program on Jewish comedians, and they could ride in a long parade. It is hard to imagine a two-hour program on Arab humor or that of any other minority group.

It is possible that Europe has been weak in the second half of the twentieth century because of the elimination of so many of its Jewish people. Not to be chauvinistic, but the Jews in some cases were the cream of societies in Europe as far as intellectual contributions went. Germany may have been first among those, ironically enough.

Prejudice against the Jews is common everywhere, including contemporary America, where the country club mentality sees them as less worthy associates. Is it Jewish exclusivity or Gentile bias that causes these troubles? Jews have had to build their own country clubs and their own "YMCAs." The author attended a YM&WHA while growing up. (That is Young Men & Women's Hebrew Association, a duplicate of the YMCA built with Jewish funds for Jewish kids.)

Jewish food is a phenomenon that is well-known in most cultures. In America, the famous delicatessens are seldom really kosher, but simply serve an Eastern European diet associated with the Jewish ghettos. Delectable "gourmet" items like corn beef and pastrami originally came from salted meats being preserved by people with no access to refrigerators. Jewish ghetto poverty has led to some interesting invention. But here again, prejudice of a peculiar kind can happen. The Orthodox look down on such restaurants. An Israeli restaurant, owned and operated by immigrant Messianic Israelis in Dallas, was closed by five rabbis who took an ad in the *Texas Jewish Post*. They simply said that they did not recommend the delicatessen, and virtually all of its Jewish business dropped. Of course, what they found so unpalatable was the belief in the Messiah, not the food. It is doubtful those rabbis ate perfectly kosher themselves. We ran an article about this situation entitled "Rabbi, Why Do You Hate Me?" in our ministry newsletter. One reader, in response to the article, travelled from Tennessee to have lunch at this delicatessen, but the place eventually closed all the same.

The "kosher" concept is unique to Jews (although various other groups do observe some dietary restrictions), and stems from the dietary laws given by God through Moses. Here again, though, Jewish law has departed from the intent of Scripture to the extent that the modern practice is almost incomprehensible when compared to its original form. A central element of kosher observance is the total separation of meat and dairy products, which can be traced back to the command in Exodus 23:19 that forbids cooking a baby goat in its mother's milk. Dr. Thomas McCall, our staff theologian, wrote his theological dissertation on sacrifices in various cultures, and he noted that pagans sacrificed in this rather cruel manner, and that is why Jews were told not to do this.

But religious leaders have embellished on this command to the point that meat and dairy products cannot be served in the same meal or prepared with the same dishes. The dishes themselves must be segregated, and kept in separate cupboards or in different areas of the house. In some Orthodox homes, there are even two dishwashers — one to wash "meat" dishes and one for "dairy" dishes, so that the two do not ever come near each other. An Orthodox Jewish woman must have four sets of dishes: one set each for dairy and meat, as well as one set each for the Passover meat and dairy dishes (which can only be used during Passover). This particular kosher practice has led to two kinds of restaurants for observant Jews, one that abstains from dairy foods and one that abstains from meat. Or if separate buildings are not possible, some restaurants have a line drawn on the floor or a rope strung across, with one side serving meat and the other side serving milk products. Even those Jews who do not follow other kosher laws will often observe this particular prohibition. For instance, my mother never served milk with our bacon.

I am not writing against the observance of the dietary laws given through Moses, which concern clean and unclean animals. God had good reason for commanding His people in this way, as modern nutritionists have certainly discovered. But this particular observance is an extreme example of what happens when people do not understand the Scripture. Following all the myriad laws of the Talmud can give an outward show of holiness, and can persuade people that they are righteous before God; but as Scripture itself has it, it is the heart that is important to God. As Jesus said to the religious leaders of His day, "Woe unto you, scribes and Pharisees, hypocrites! for ye make clean the outside of the cup and of the platter, but within they are full of extortion and excess" (Matt. 23:25).

Lack of sound Bible knowledge creates some new kind of Jewish manners and mores. There is an odd kind of Judaism that looks forward to End

Times prophecy, particularly the Temple rebuilding, even as it omits the rest of Bible study. There are Jewish people in Israel making costumes for worship in the new Temple, jewelry for the women to wear, and trumpets to be blown to herald the services. These activities celebrate Scripture, and yet the rest of biblical Judaism is of little importance to this sect. Israel by itself presents some amazing Jewish stories. In some cases, the Orthodox living there have recreated their European ghettos, albeit in nicer surroundings, by wearing the costumes and copying the manners and mores of those three and four-hundred-year-old societies. Little boys wear skullcaps and forelocks. Orthodox women shave their heads in submission when they marry (and then buy the finest, most elaborate wigs available, along with expensive, florid hats). At the same time, a family living right across the street may detest these mannerisms and look down on all Judaism as a relic and irrelevant. Still another family might try to affect a "sensible" middle ground, worshipping on holidays but otherwise taking a secular, Zionistic view of Israel. It should not be thought that all of the Orthodox are supportive of Israel. Many of them believe the place should not be occupied by Jews until the Messiah comes, and they are actually anti-Israeli, to the extreme of even drawing swastikas on walls to represent the government as being tyrannical like the Nazis were! Most will not use the Hebrew language, and consequently speak the Yiddish of the ghettos, a re-markable rebirth of an agonizing period in the long story of Judaism.

The question of real faith is complex. I once sat at a Sabbath dinner in Jerusalem where I marvelled at the speed with which the family slammed their way through the prayers at the table. I could not help but point out that God Himself would have trouble understanding the diction when people were reading like auctioneers, and my hostess began talking about her beliefs. Ultimately she said, "I don't have to believe in anything, I just have to read these prayers." That is an extreme statement of how law overcomes faith and works are the whole religion.

The manners and mores of a four-thousand-year-old people are impossible to explain in this space, of course, and I hardly think I have done them justice. But it should be appreciated that there is something called the Jewish way, which operates in the Jewish community and has always done so, from the ancient days to the present. That peculiar Jewish style exists from the Old City of Jerusalem to the Warsaw ghetto to Brooklyn to the New City of Jerusalem, and is always a separated society, rich in lore, poetry, music, art, etc., but totally sealed off from both the Jewish and the Gentile sides. The wall separating Jews and Gentiles seems to have a plaster surface on either side and the issue of each other's faith is barely understood at all.

And finally, the manners and mores of the Jewish people are simply not based on the Bible. That is remarkable since, as we have pointed out, the Bible is wholly a Jewish book. One would hardly expect sacrifices to be done in an age when there is no valid temple in Jerusalem to receive them, of course, but the Bible (or at least the Old Testament) has its own Jewish style, which simply no longer appears. Devoutness is a concept which is simply not seen in the Jewish community; rather, there is adherence to Talmudic law and obedience to European patterns of worship. Simple belief in God seems to be lacking. Worldliness, condemned throughout Scripture, is considered almost a virtue in the Jewish community.

Once again, the error is concerned with lack of Bible knowledge.

Chapter 5. The Synagogue

I must admit that it has been some years since I regularly attended a synagogue, a statement that might well be made by a majority of adult Jewish people. When I do go back from time to time, I find little changed from my boyhood. The same strengths are there: unparalleled pageantry and beauty, a rabbi who usually has intelligence and wit, and a certain sincerity of worship, at least in the Orthodox and Conservative branches. But the same weaknesses are there also: a liturgy out of touch with Scripture, a stress on ceremony to the exclusion of understanding, and an emphasis on fine dress and religious mannerisms.

Gentiles would find the synagogue odd indeed. Although they would see so much variety that they would hardly think there was any consistent norm.

Jewish synagogues vary from storefronts where the Orthodox do their peculiar and virtually all-Hebrew worship, to grand auditoriums where the Reform hold lectures and high holiday pageants. Some synagogues have grand choirs and organs, some are spartan. Common to them all is the rabbi, whom we have described previously.

The rabbi is the outstanding feature of the synagogue, as the minister is of the church. And in the synagogue, too, the clergy presents an overwhelming variation of talent, knowledge and sincerity. We have touched on the idea (in chapter five of the first section) that the rabbi in his present form is an invention of the post-biblical times. There was no sermonizing, congregational leader in the Temples of old. The synagogue had more of an administrator than a spiritual leader. Though many rabbis are most conscientious in what they see their work to be, there seems to be no definition that holds from community to community of what this office entails. One could just as well run into a woman in her twenties, freshly graduated from a progressive seminary, as the classical white-haired sage of yore. The rabbi of a given synagogue may be deeply involved with God, or at least with Talmud and the Jewish law, or he may agnostic, seeking only to organize his congregation around a concept of Jewish community. A small percentage of rabbis even claim to be atheists, making a great deal of the fact that they are worldly leaders indeed, not given to hoary religious traditions of ancient days. The rabbis do tend to follow their "denominational" lines, the Reform being quite liberal, the Conservative in the middle, and the Orthodox very given to ritual worship and study of the law. All venerate the Torah in proportion to their denominational calling, but if the truth be told, literal Bible study is simply not done. It is rather the commentaries on the Torah and the rest of the Old Testament that are studied. The most Orthodox of rabbis would not be a match for an ordinary Christian seminary student when it comes to verse-by-verse Bible study.

The synagogues are filled most completely on the high holidays: the Feast of Trumpets, the Day of Atonement, and the Feast of Tabernacles. (As given in Torah — Leviticus 23:24, 27 & 34 respectively.) The Feast of Trumpets has lost its meaning in Torah (Lev. 23:24; compare with Lev. 25:10, etc.). It is simply regarded as the new year and called Rosh Hashanah, literally the head or beginning of the year. The Torah specifies, however, that Nisan, the month of Passover, is the beginning of the year (see Exodus 12:2). Jewish tradition established different kinds of years, including ceremonial years, a planting year, etc. As a practical matter, it was probably found that more people would attend services in the fall, when the harvest was in, than in other parts of the festival year, and little by little the Feast of Trumpets became New Year's Day.

The Jewish people pay for their seats in the synagogue, rather than passing a collection plate. When I was a youngster, we received a regular invoice billing us for our particular seats — the same from year to year — for the high holidays. The rest of the year was "free of charge" and we could attend on any Sabbath or other festival. There is little question that synagogues receive excellent support and normally can undertake building programs and the sponsorship of orphans and old folks homes and the like with confidence.

The system of "billing" surprises Christians as much as the system of collection plates surprises Jews, but both systems seem to be working well, at least where there is enough of a community of believers to support the building and the clergy.

We have talked about the Orthodox-Conservative-Reform differences several times before, but in regard to the synagogue, the differences are profound. A stranger to Jewish culture would be hard-pressed to place the average Reform congregation in the same religion with the average Orthodox congregation. Only a few artifacts around the room might be the same (if the Reform has a menorah, a Torah, or other symbols of the faith). The Orthodox would seem disorganized and busy, with their central pulpit crowded with those reading Scripture and those who have been honored with introductory readings; and the congregation itself would be reading prayer books, praying, or even conversing as the service clattered on. The Reform would look more like a denominational Protestant church, with proper decorum. There would be a front platform with a speaker holding forth, and probably a choir. The service would be built around the message of the rabbi, and that message would more likely concern modern life or the Jewish condition in some form rather than Scripture. A Conservative synagogue would fit neatly between the two, with the front platform containing the Scripture reader and others in the congregation doing some of the decorous prayers and some of the milling and individual readings. (It should be stressed that the breakdown of Judaism into these three major groups is very largely a phenomenon of the Western world. Jews from Europe, Russia and the Mediterranean area would only recognize the Orthodox. In Israel, the Orthodox totally predominate, dictating all matters of Jewish law and recognizing no conversions, marriages, etc., done by the other denominations.)

What all these factions have in common, again, is the utter lack of biblical content. It could not be said that the services lack spiritual content, because there is something very spiritual indeed in the reciting of the ancient prayers and in the willingness of the people to be there and to participate. A truly biblical person would find the services weak in meaty scriptural concepts, of course, but the biblically-unread layman is won over by the pageantry and the effort of it all. But whatever complaints a biblical person might make of synagogues, it is a fact that they hold together very well and they do a good job of what they are doing. Israel receives support, the Russian Jews are rescued and welcomed into Israel, and the charity called the United Jewish Appeal runs third in the United States, behind only the Salvation Army and the American Red Cross, as a fundraising source. That is exceedingly impressive when one considers that the Jews make up about two percent of American society, at the most. If the American Heart Association and the Cancer Society had the willing donors of the United Jewish Appeal, these diseases might well have been conquered by now.

Although weekly attendance is not compulsory, it would be impossible to discuss the synagogue without also considering the Sabbath. The Sabbath is a biblical concept that has not escaped the Jews. In fact, they are among the few groups in the world actually celebrating a Saturday Sabbath, which is what the Old Testament calls for. On the other hand, the Jews tend to overdo the meaning of the Sabbath. The Orthodox, especially, add an out-of-proportion emphasis to this particular observance. It has become the strangest exaggeration of the intention of Scripture. While the Bible makes clear that there is to be a day of rest and gives good reason for it, the Talmud makes this an onerous requirement indeed. One must not turn on a light, start a car or press an elevator button due to prohibitions against kindling a fire on the Sabbath. (It stands to reason that this prohibition was instituted because the gathering of wood would have violated the law against working on the Sabbath, but rabbis have ruled that igniting any spark violates this law.) And so, in hotels and other tall buildings in Israel, there is at least one "Sabbath elevator" that on Friday nights and Saturdays will run up and down continuously, stopping automatically on each floor, so that observant Jews can use it without having to violate the law by pressing the buttons! Doors that open electronically throughout the week have a tendency to break noses when they are disconnected on the Sabbath and people forget that they are not working.

Although there are laws against driving on the Sabbath, there are some Jews who manage to get around them. There is an Orthodox synagogue around the corner from my house. People may drive there for evening services, but on Friday evening a chain goes up and all cars parked there are essentially impounded until Saturday evening, when the chain comes down and people are again free to drive them home. In the meantime, all services must be attended on foot. But I recently noticed that some of the members have been parking their cars behind my house on the Sabbath, and then proceeding on foot, with proper decorum, to the synagogue. After the service, they leave the synagogue on foot and walk with great dignity until they are out of sight around the corner, and then get in their cars and drive home.

Ethiopian Jews choose to sit in the dark on the Sabbath. The Orthodox have told them that they can bring in a "Shabbas Goy" (literally a "Sabbath Gentile," a non-Jew who is friendly to the family) to turn on the lights for them; but the Ethiopians have seen the many techniques the Orthodox Jews use to skirt their myriad Sabbath laws, and they have replied, "We know the ways to get around the law; we are trying to keep it."

Cars are not used and buses do not operate in Jerusalem on the Sabbath, and the distance that one may walk is limited as well. However, someone had the bright idea of creating an "aruv," which is a bordered area within which one may walk extra distances on the Sabbath (such as the courtyard of an apartment building). I have heard it said that there is an aruv, a hypothetical string, around the whole city of Jerusalem! One may wear a coat, but he cannot carry it. I could go on and on. The point is that rampant legalism has overtaken a simple scriptural law — a phenomenon that occurs whenever anyone, Christian or Jew, gets away from the Bible as the sole foundation for the practice of his faith.

Chapter 6. Prophecy

Where prophecy is concerned, it is simply unknown to modern Jewish worship and practice. The Jews simply do not appreciate that Scripture is full of prophecy and that a huge section of the Tenach (the Old Testament) is called Navi'im, or Prophets. They may know that title and they may actually use the term prophet, but they do not understand that men inspired of God literally predicted future events, and that some of those events are still being fulfilled for Jewish people today, most notably the restoration of Israel. We alluded to this amazing lack in Judaism in the first chapter of this section. The Jews, among all peoples, should understand prophecy, since it concerns three issues deeply involved with Judaism: the Land, the Messiah and the end of times.

The Old Testament is simply replete with Messianic prophecy, which creates a kind of embarrassment for Jewish people trying to refute "the missionaries." There are whole schools of Jewish thought on how to wriggle out of obvious prophecies of Christ, such as Isaiah 53, Daniel 9:24-27, Micah 5:2, etc. That the Messiah was to be born in Bethlehem in the first century of the Tribe of Judah is Old Testament Scripture and that is all there is to that. The prophets have clearly stated it, but it is totally ignored. Rather, ingenious ways are found to escape the clear meaning of the verses so that Jesus is avoided.

The consulting theologian of this ministry, Dr. Thomas S. McCall, once argued Messianic prophecy with a particularly adept expostulator, who was able to evade each and every prophecy that Dr. McCall could bring up. The discussion went on and on until Dr. McCall had virtually finished all Messianic prophecies in the Old Testament, at which point he inquired, "By the way, where did you people ever get the idea that a Messiah was coming in the first place?"

A great deal of prophecy about the nation of Israel is also missed, so that even the Israelis are many times unaware that they have the Land because of a divine land grant. And finally, the prophecies of the end are crucial.

Considering that one third of the Bible is prophecy and that all prophecy, especially that of the End Times, concerns the Jews, it simply astonishing that the synagogues have no knowledge of it and virtually never mention it.

Probably a lot that I have said in this book has been irritating to many people. I have tried to be as factual and evenhanded as possible in discussing the two faiths with which I am familiar. It is not an easy thing, frankly, for me to criticize either one. I grew up a Jew and will always be a Jew and, though constantly maligned by my Jewish brethren, that is how I am and how virtually all Jews are. We never convert to something else and we do not change our Jewishness. (Even in the case of forced conversions in Medieval times, the Jewish identity remained in most of those people. Truly biblical converts to Christ could never lose their Judaism, but rather they become much more related to a greater Judaism.) My Christian experience re-routed my entire life from a given point in so remarkable a way that my original prayer — "if you're there, show me" — has certainly been answered again and again, and is still answered every day. So I do not mean to really criticize either faith, but to enhance understanding of what might be done to help with the trouble with Christians and the trouble with Jews.

Here are some suggestions, offered with humility.

1. Teach Salvation

It would seem too obvious to tell the churches to teach the doctrine of salvation, and impertinent to teach it to Jews. But frankly, this is the first lack in both camps.

Most of the Christian church is "liberal," by which most people mean there is no personal relationship with Christ urged on people and no "moment of salvation." When interviewing employees at our ministry, we usually ask the question, "When were you saved?" The answers come in quite a variety, most of the applicants trying to appear very Christian indeed, to make us as happy as possible with their reply. Those who attended churches which did not teach the doctrine of salvation will usually make a speech of several paragraphs involving their lifelong church attendance, good works, etc., etc., but not coming to the point of a specific time of salvation. Solid, born-again believers simply answer, "March 14, 1971" (as in my case). Non-Christian people will tend to say, "I have always believed that there is a Lord-like spirit upon us all," or some such worldly pleasantry.

What needs to be taught in the churches is that people must individually come to Christ in prayer and ask for His salvation. They must first know who He is by reading His teachings or hearing of them told accurately, and they must ask Him individually to be saved. Or as the Lord instructed the Samaritan woman in John 4:10 in a single statement:

If thou knewest the gift of God, and who it is that saith to thee, Give me to drink;

thou wouldest have asked of him, and he would have given thee living water.

As to the Jews, it might seem extraordinary that they would ever teach a doctrine called salvation, but they might regard it in another way. It is the relationship with God that is in question here, and that is the point at which modern Judaism seems weak. If the characters of the Bible spoke to God and believed in Him, and if He is so revered among modern Jews that one cannot write down His name or even say it, then He is certainly worth "knowing." It may appear presumptuous to the modern Jewish person that he could have a "personal relationship" with so powerful and seemingly remote a God, but Scripture is full of that and every Jew knows in his heart that when he prays, he pictures a listening and responsive heavenly God. Closeness to that God is the issue, and more or less parallels Christian salvation. If pursuing a personal relationship to God the Father might draw a Jewish person to investigate closeness to the Messiah, no harm will be done.

In any case, in both the liberal churches and all of the synagogues, some discussion of the relationship between man and his God should take place.

2. Teach About the Messiah

Both the Christians and the Jews could stand

much more information about the Messiah, whichever Messiah they have in mind.

As to the Christians, we have reviewed their polyglot estimations of Jesus Christ. The different denominations see so remarkably different a Messiah that is no wonder that they cannot find common ground. What needs to be taught is the word-for-word teachings of Christ in the Gospels, nothing more, nothing less. Commentary might be helpful, but Scripture is Scripture. Pastors need to learn to quote Jesus word-for-word, and not merely make homilies of what they suppose He said. The laity needs to read the Bible every day, most intensively the Gospels so that they understand the One they worship.

In the synagogues, teachings about Messiah are crucial, as this is a central doctrine of Judaism almost totally misunderstood. For an Orthodox group to choose Rabbi Schneerson, or for the Jews to follow Bar Kochba, or Sabbatiel, could never have happened if the simple descriptions of the Messiah available throughout the Old Testament were heeded. None of those three satisfied any of Isaiah 53, the "suffering servant" chapter, or the precepts of Daniel 9, that the Messiah would appear before the destruction of the Temple (in the Christian reading). I do not mean to say that the Messianic prophecies must necessarily be read in a Christological sense. They can be read in a general sense with an open mind about who the Messiah might someday be, but in any case they ought to be read! If the Jewish idea of the Messiah is whatever story was passed on from village to village in the old country, the Jews would of course have no idea who He was when He came. The rabbis have drifted so far apart on this subject, that one finally said in *Time* magazine a few years ago that if, when the Messiah comes, He turns out to be Jesus, that would be perfectly okay.

I am not appealing that we teach Jesus in the synagogues, but only that we teach about the Messiah as He is given in Old Testament Scripture. Who He is must, as always, be up to each individual person once he masters the scriptural descriptions.

3. Prophecy

It goes without saying that the synagogue must begin to study prophecy, like the church should, or both will be completely confounded by all that is coming up. Prophecy is "batting a thousand." All predicted events have come about in their due course, if Scripture is to be believed, and therefore we should be able to rely on End Times prophecy.

It would belabor the point to emphasize how crucial this study would be in both the synagogue and the church. The synagogue will certainly not wish to open the New Testament on this subject, but that is not necessary. The vast majority of prophetic statements are found in the Old Testament, and at the very least, Jews should be knowledgeable of these messages of such historical importance. It goes without saying that names like Daniel, Isaiah, Jeremiah, and so forth, are better known in this world than Homer, Plato, Aristotle, etc., and if the truth be told, more valued by more people.

4. Israel

One major trouble with both the Christians and the Jews is that neither group understands Israel in a biblical sense. We have alluded to this subject above, but it should be said here that without both groups understanding Israel as a fulfillment of prophecy, the Bible becomes incomprehensible.

Israel is a nation in a modern sense, and seems to have come about by geopolitical means in the modern world. But with that said, it should be seen by spiritual people also as the most remarkable fulfillment of prophecy in our time. If we consider the following verses against the modern situation, it will be seen that a prophecy of a range of 3,500 years is being perfectly fulfilled!

And it shall come to pass, when all these things are come upon thee, the blessing and the curse, which I have set before thee, and thou shalt call them to mind among all the nations, whither the Lord thy God hath driven thee, and shalt return unto the Lord thy God, and shalt obey his voice according to all that I command thee this day, thou and thy children, with all thine heart, and with all thy soul; that then the Lord thy God will turn thy captivity, and have compassion upon thee, and will return and gather thee from all the nations, whither the Lord thy God hath scattered thee. If any of thine be driven out unto the outmost parts of heaven, from thence will the Lord thy God gather thee, and from thence will he fetch thee: and the Lord thy God will bring thee into the land which thy fathers possessed, and thou shalt possess it; and he will do thee good, and multiply thee above thy fathers. (Deuteronomy 30:1-5)

Both Christians and Jews can appreciate that Torah reference, and they need to. Jewish people who are anti-Israel (and there are plenty) are simply anti-Torah. Christian people who are anti-Israel (and there are plenty) are anti-Scripture. That is all there is to that.

Many more suggestions might be made in the service of enhancing the spiritual condition of both Christians and Jews, but let me try to wrap it up in one simple formula:

We must all read the Bible.

Appendix A: A Christian Example

Replacement Theology

A major problem with Christian people not individually reading the Bible is that they fall into false doctrines. They are a ready audience for an enterprising teacher to capture. Those Christians who do not particularly like Jews, and there are a few, have come up with any number of ways to disenfranchise the Chosen People. The most popular and widespread is replacement theology. This is a doctrine so detached from Scripture that only people who have really never picked up a Bible would fall into it. That unfortunately includes a great many "Christians."

The following material is taken from my book *Broken Branches*, a short discussion of replacement theology. Let it serve as a practical example of how far lack of Bible reading can take one from the Bible.

If some of the branches have been broken off, and you, though a wild olive shoot, have been grafted in among the others and now share in the nourishing sap from the olive root, do not boast over those branches. If you do, consider this: You do not support the root, but the root supports you. (Romans 11:17-18, NIV)

Our subject is replacement theology, a doctrine that has been around almost as long as the church has been in existence. Its adherents say that since Israel was "broken off" because of its rejection of the Messiah, it has been replaced by the church. All of God's promises to Israel from the Old Testament, including God's covenant with Abraham, would then apply to the church rather than to Abraham's descendants.

Have the Jews as the Chosen People, the nation of Israel fathered by Abraham, been replaced by the church? Does it no longer have any part in God's plan? If the Jews have lost their unique place in God's plan as descendants of Abraham, can a Jew become a Christian and still be a Jew, or would he then be a Gentile? Replacement theology has led to much confusion on these and other issues.

In reality, the church is an organization of both Jews and Gentiles who believe in Jesus Christ, today as it always was. It may seem to onlookers that Gentile Christians have utterly taken over the faith in the Jewish Messiah, but as Paul points out in Romans 11, there has always been a remnant of Jews in the church. Replacement theologians make the error of seeing the church as different than it is. They seem to regard it as a result of the salvation of Gentiles and divorced from its original Jewish heritage. But the salvation of the Gentiles in the first place was a Jewish mission. Jews were the first Christians and they carried their blessing to the Gentiles among them, as was the will of God.

The church seems entirely Gentile, because after all, every church is just packed with Gentiles. But if we examine the Bible and the birth of the church, a very different picture emerges than the one painted by replacement theologians.

I want to start with the whole issue of Gentile salvation, beginning with its history. It did not start in the same way as the salvation of the Jews. During His work on earth, the Lord witnessed to a handful of Gentiles and a few were saved. The people of the town of the Samaritan woman certainly were saved (John 4), as well as the Phoenician woman whose daughter was vexed with a devil (Matthew 15) and the Roman officer whose servant was healed by the Lord (Matthew 8). But other than the few extraordinary cases, the Lord's ministry was to the Jews. In fact, He instructed His disciples as follows:

> *Go not into the way of the Gentiles, and into any city of the Samaritans enter ye not: but go rather to the lost sheep of the house of Israel. (Matthew 10:5-6)*

On the whole, Gentile salvation waited until the book of Acts and the career of Peter, who was really the Apostle to the Jews. He had preached the sermon at Pentecost in Acts 2, where 3,000 Jews were saved, and with John healed the lame man at the Temple gate (Acts 3:1 - 4:4), winning another 5,000 souls!

But on one significant occasion, Peter was called to a Gentile household. I refer to Acts 10, where it says:

> *There was a certain man in Caesarea*
> *called Cornelius, a centurion of the band*
> *called the Italian band. . . . (vs. 1)*

Cornelius was an officer in the Roman army, and yet he was a devout man, as stated in verse 2:

> *A devout man, and one that feared God*
> *with all his house, which gave much alms*
> *to the people, and prayed to God alway.*

He may have been one of the halfway converts to Judaism, those people who did not undertake mikvah (ritual bathing) and circumcision, but who did follow certain Jewish practices. They came to the worship services and watched what went on, and they admired Judaism and did not worship the Roman gods, who had all too human attributes and foibles. They went to the real God of Judaism, which took them in the direction of the real Messiah. Cornelius had a dream to send for Peter, and that Apostle, the great fisherman, came to his house.

> *And as he talked with him, he went in,*

and found many that were come together.
And he said unto them, Ye know how that
it is an unlawful thing for a man that is a
Jew to keep company, or come unto one
of another nation; but God hath showed
me that I should not call any man com-
mon or unclean. (vss. 27-28)

According to ancient Jewish law, Peter should
not have fraternized with Gentiles so closely as
to visit in their homes, eat with them, and so forth.
Yet here he was, associating with them. He said:

Therefore came I unto you without gain-
saying, as soon as I was sent for: I ask
therefore for what intent ye have sent for
me? (vs. 29)

Cornelius then described his dream and the
specific instructions he was given to send for Peter.

Then Peter opened his mouth, and said,
Of a truth I perceive that God is no re-
specter of persons: But in every nation he
that feareth him, and worketh righteous-
ness, is accepted with him. (vss. 34-35)

"God is no respecter of persons" has often
been used by Caucasians to allow non-whites to
come into the church — blacks, Hispanics, even

Jews. Actually, it was originally to allow the white Europeans in! The church started, of course, in Israel and here was a case of a Roman officer and his friends, a group of Europeans, hearing the Gospel for the first time. Peter shared it with them, and then:

> *While Peter yet spake these words, the Holy Ghost fell on all them which heard the word. (vs. 44)*

Amazing! The Gentiles began to praise God. The Jewish believers who had come with Peter could hardly believe their eyes.

> *And they of the circumcision which believed were astonished, as many as came with Peter, because that on the Gentiles also was poured out the gift of the Holy Ghost. (vs. 45)*

This was something new to them. They had seen the Lord witness to the occasional Gentile, as I pointed out earlier, but by and large Christ's mission was to the Jews and was a fulfillment of Jewish prophecy and law. It had probably never occurred to them that Gentiles could believe in the Jewish Messiah.

It is thought-provoking that in Acts, the church fathers in Jerusalem (the "Messianic congregation" of that time) took issue with Peter when he returned from his meeting with Cornelius.

And when Peter was come up to Jerusalem, they that were of the circumcision contended with him, Saying, Thou wentest in to men uncircumcised, and didst eat with them. (Acts 11:2-3)

It is as if they were saying, "Great fisherman, friend of Jesus, you preached the sermon at Pentecost and led 3,000 people to Christ! You were instrumental when 5,000 were saved at the Temple gate. But still, you went into a Roman household, you talked to Roman officers about Jesus Christ! Do you think Gentiles can hear this and understand it and come to our Jewish Messiah?" So Peter explained the dream that God sent to teach him that he should not call anything unclean:

But the voice answered me again from heaven, What God hath cleansed, that call not thou common. (vs. 9)

Obviously, God had extended the Gospel to the Gentiles. There is actually a proof text for it. There is a certain game that I play in churches that I visit. I say to people, "You're so certain of Gentile salvation. Give me a verse that tells me that Gentiles can be saved. I have a thousand verses in the Gospels that say Jews can be saved."

They think it is almost a joke, and yet they cannot find a verse to support Gentile salvation. Try this one:

> *When they heard these things, they held*
> *their peace, and glorified God, saying,*
> *Then hath God also to the Gentiles*
> *granted repentance unto life. (vs. 18)*

It is that simple. Gentiles are invited. Everyone is invited. When John the Baptist saw Jesus coming, he said, "Behold the Lamb of God, which taketh away the sin *of the world*" (John 1:29). Not *of Israel*, which would have been logical for him to say, since only Israel was under the law. No, salvation in Christ is for all, the death of Christ was for all, and the whole wide world is forgiven through the sacrifice of Christ. In this passage in Acts, we see it as it was starting to happen. This is the beginning of the history of Gentile salvation, at the home of Cornelius in Caesarea, a city located along the Mediterranean coast north of Tel Aviv and south of Haifa. The ruins of this city are still there and we visit them on our tours of Israel.

After the Jerusalem Christians had heard Peter's report and accepted that God's salvation is also for the Gentiles, the very next verse says:

> *Now they which were scattered abroad*
> *upon the persecution that arose about*

Stephen travelled as far as Phenice, and Cyprus, and Antioch, preaching the word to none but unto the Jews only. (vs. 19)

Stephen was the Apostle who was stoned in Jerusalem. The Messianic Jews were hated and feared by the Temple priesthood, which persecuted and scattered the young church. The Christians on the road did not know about the conversion of Cornelius and Peter's report to Jerusalem, so they continued to preach only to the Jews. When they came to a town, they would go to its synagogue. Paul did this throughout his career. When he arrived in Athens, he witnessed at the synagogue. In Asia, or what we call Turkey today, in the towns of the seven churches and others that Paul visited, he went first to the Jews, who would be interested to hear a rabbi from Israel — especially if he could report that the Messiah had come. At the least, they would want to evaluate such a claim. The Greeks would have no interest in this subject. So the scattered believers took the Gospel first to the Jews alone. And a few verses later in Acts 11, we find that:

. . . the disciples were called Christians first in Antioch. (vs. 26)

If they were called "Christians" first in Antioch, and if the people that went to Antioch were "preaching the word to none but unto the

Jews only" (Acts 11:19), then all the people who
were first called Christians were Jews! So, when
the history of Gentile salvation started, there were
already many Christian Jews. The Christian
church was well underway by the time Cornelius
and his household were saved.

About this time, the great missionary Paul was
converted and set about spreading the Gospel and
establishing churches throughout the Roman empire. Christianity grew until, a few centuries down
the road, a major error came into the church. St.
Augustine wrote a treatise called *The City of God*,
in which he concluded that God was through with
Israel and the church was its replacement. This
was the start of replacement theology as a church
doctrine.

Did Augustine write this out of malice or anti-
Semitism? Did he dislike the Jews? Not necessarily. The Jews had been dispersed. The Romans raided Israel in 70 A.D. and again in 135
A.D. and the Jews fled far and wide. At the time
of Augustine, there just was not a Jewish Israel to
be seen. Even the name of the Land was changed
in 135 A.D. to Palestine — "Philistia," after the
Philistines. (This name had nothing whatsoever
to do with Arab peoples. The Moslems weren't
to come on the scene for 500 years. The Romans
renamed the Land to wipe out Judaism. It was
another of those "final solutions" to the Jewish
problem. Today, we are hearing the preposterous
idea that Arab Moslems are the original Palestin-

ians. This is not only nonsense, it is crazier than nonsense.)

It wasn't long before the church picked up on Augustine's doctrine, and the original Catholic church began to think that it was Israel. This belief became a tenet of the church and was carried down through the centuries. However it started, it became an anti-Jewish doctrine which cut Israel and the Jews completely out of Christianity, even though they were the original Christians!

Roman Catholicism eventually led to the Reformation. Martin Luther called on fellow Christians to return to the Scriptures. And some of them did. They realized that the Scriptures were better than priests selling indulgences, and crusades and inquisitions, and other unbiblical burdens. But even though they returned to the Scriptures, somehow they continued the error of replacement theology. To them, the Jews were just some people who lived in the ghetto on the wrong side of town. Having been raised to view them as a disadvantaged minority with nothing to say about Christ, the Gentile Christians could not believe that they ought to seriously consider Israel. By the time of the Reformation, Israel as a country had not been in existence for almost 1500 years. It seemed like forever since Jews lived in the Land.

And so the error of replacement theology continued. Over time, Christians split into denominations, with each one splintering into other sects until there are now something like 300 Christian denominations just in America. (One of the hard things in witnessing to Jews is when they ask, "Just which brand of Christianity would you like me to embrace?" That's a tough question.) But lately, there has been a new movement. I would almost call it a new Reformation or a neo-Reformation which has given birth to what are called "Bible churches." These churches get back to verse-by-verse study of the Scriptures. The Rapture has been uncovered and a greater theological understanding has come out of this. These churches reject replacement theology. They are actively involved with Israel. They have read the prophecies and are excited by the fact that God has brought the Jews back to the Land.

Israel is crucial. It is God's timepiece. The true Bible churches study the Scriptures and not old doctrines, and so they avoid mistakes like replacement theology. They read the Abrahamic Covenant correctly:

> *And I will establish my covenant between me and thee and thy seed after thee in their generations for an everlasting covenant, to be a God unto thee, and to thy seed after thee. And I will give unto thee, and to thy seed after thee, the land wherein thou art a stranger, all the land of Canaan, for an everlasting possession; and I will be their God. (Genesis 17:7-8)*

When God established an "everlasting" covenant, it is impossible to say that somewhere down the line the Jews misbehaved and caused the covenant to be broken. God Himself said, "*olam*," which means "everlasting" in Hebrew. It is forever, complete, done, universal.

God's promise included all the land of Canaan. This is the sort of promise that those who study the Bible can appreciate. God means something when He says "everlasting." It will not vary; it will not end. Even though the Jews were later dispersed from the Land, we are seeing the fulfillment of God's covenant today:

> *That then the LORD thy God will turn thy captivity, and have compassion upon thee, and will return and gather thee from all the nations, whither the LORD thy God hath scattered thee. If any of thine be driven out unto the outmost parts of heaven, from thence will the LORD thy God gather thee, and from thence will he fetch thee: And the LORD thy God will bring thee into the land which thy fathers possessed, and thou shalt possess it; and he will do thee good, and multiply thee above thy fathers. (Deuteronomy 30:3-5)*

No one — no one! — can read that passage and look at Israel and not think, "those two go together." I don't care if he is the latest theologian to write about replacement theology, he cannot escape this promise. There is a compelling parallel between God saying, "Even if you were driven to the outmost parts of heaven" (that is, all over creation) and the phenomenon today of Jews being brought back to the Land from Ethiopia, from Russia, from America, from South America, from practically everywhere but the South Pole. If you think that there is no correspondence between these two occurrences, you might as well just throw the Bible away.

The dry bones vision in Ezekiel 37 also backs this up:

Then he said unto me, Son of man, these bones are the whole house of Israel: behold, they say, Our bones are dried, and our hope is lost: we are cut off for our parts.

Therefore prophesy and say unto them, Thus saith the Lord GOD; Behold, O my people, I will open your graves, and cause you to come up out of your graves, and bring you into the land of Israel.

And ye shall know that I am the LORD, when I have opened your graves, O my people, and brought you up out of your graves,

*And shall put my spirit in you, and ye shall
live, and I shall place you in your own
land: then shall ye know that I the LORD
have spoken it, and performed it, saith the
LORD. (vss. 11-14)*

God says, "You're out there in Gentile lands,
but I will open those graves and bring you back."
That is a powerful image. "You thought you were
dying out there, and I will bring you back into
your own land, make you spiritual again, and then
the kingdom will come." That is the point of the
dry bones vision. Bone connects to bone, flesh
to flesh as they build up. Then they take a breath,
and the spirit comes into them, and they are whole.
They are the true Israel restored.

We are in the middle of this today. We are
seeing it happen. If someone says, "Israel doesn't
count," it does not matter how many degrees he
has, either he has to be wrong or the Bible is
wrong. This is very personal with God. His love
for Israel is not a casual thing. Defending Israel
against mindless media bias, against the Moslems,
especially against the replacement theologians, is
very important to me and should be important to
every believer. Israel will be our kingdom! We
are going there for a thousand years. You could
spend your whole life saying, "Israel doesn't
count, Israel doesn't count," but you will end up
standing there in Jerusalem with your King.

If Israel's behavior was bad, does it mean that
God would turn His back on them? They dis-
obeyed God out in the wilderness. The context
in Leviticus 26 is chastisements, one after another:

> *But if ye will not hearken unto me, and
> will not do all these commandments; And
> if ye shall despise my statutes, or if your
> soul abhor my judgments, so that ye will
> not do all my commandments, but that ye
> break my covenant. . . . (Leviticus 26:14-
> 15)*

God is angry. But, beginning in verse 44, He
says:

> *And yet for all that, when they be in the
> land of their enemies, I will not cast them
> away, neither will I abhor them, to de-
> stroy them utterly, and to break my cov-
> enant with them: for I am the LORD their
> God. But I will for their sakes remember
> the covenant of their ancestors, whom I
> brought forth out of the land of Egypt in
> the sight of the heathen, that I might be
> their God: I am the LORD. (vss. 44-45)*

God's covenant with Israel does not depend
on their behavior, just as our salvation in Christ
does not depend on our behavior. God is not keeping score and trying to keep people out. To be

accurate, He said that He is not willing that any should perish (2 Peter 3:9). He is trying to get people in, for heaven's sake! His love for Israel, His forbearance with them, is unshakable.

There is no stronger passage about God's love for Israel than Jeremiah's announcement of the New Covenant:

> *Thus saith the LORD, which giveth the sun for a light by day, and the ordinances of the moon and of the stars for a light by night, which divideth the sea when the waves thereof roar; The LORD of hosts is his name. . . . (Jeremiah 31:35)*

God gives these ordinances and signs this covenant, and He says this:

> *If those ordinances depart from before me, saith the LORD, then the seed of Israel also shall cease from being a nation before me for ever. (vs. 36)*

The moon is still coming up and the sun is still shining. The waves still run up on the beach, therefore Israel is still a nation before the Lord.

> *Thus saith the LORD; If heaven above can be measured, and the foundations of the earth searched out beneath, I will also cast off all the seed of Israel for all that they*

have done, saith the LORD. (vs. 37)

God presented a similar situation to Job: "where were you when I laid the foundations of the earth; when I laid the cornerstone of the earth?" (Job 38:4,6) If you can tell God how the earth is hung in space, then He will agree, "O.K., I will cast off Israel." He cannot say it more strongly. Yet there are Christian scholars teaching that God has cast off Israel. They are wrong. Not right, not medium, but dead wrong.

Some people believe that the modern nation of Israel is not the same nation as the Israel of biblical times, but it is the only nation in the world today that can trace by language, by religion, by prayers and songs and costumes — by everything — that it does go back to that era. The people of Israel are the most exact picture we have from biblical times. Americans go back only 200 years; Englishmen perhaps 800 to 1,000 years. Only Israel goes back those thousands of years to the Scriptures, saying the same words every Sabbath as written there 3,500 years ago. This is the biblical Israel and you cannot cast it out. God has not cast it out.

If God takes His promises away based on behavior, then sinners cannot count on salvation in Christ either. If He must keep His promises to Christians as His people, then He must keep His covenant with Israel as well.

Paul saw the error of replacement theology in

his own time, and dealt with it in Romans 11:

> *I say then, Hath God cast away his*
> *people? God forbid. For I also am an*
> *Israelite, of the seed of Abraham, of the*
> *tribe of Benjamin. God hath not cast away*
> *his people which he foreknew. . . .*
> *(Romans 11:1-2)*

The whole chapter of Romans 11 is devoted to this very error. I wonder if replacement theologians tear this chapter out of the Bible and refuse to read it. "God hath not cast away His people which He foreknew." If He hath, tell me how He hath! I like the note for this chapter in the Scofield Study Bible: "That Israel has not been forever set aside is the theme of this chapter."

If Israel has not been "forever set aside," then what is its current relationship to God? The coming of Jesus obviously brought changes in God's dealings with His people. A right relationship with God is now available only through the salvation provided by Christ's death and resurrection. Hebrews 8:13 makes clear that a new covenant has been established and the old one is obsolete. But what is the covenant that was actually done away with? This is the source of a lot of the confusion of replacement theology. God in fact established two covenants with Israel: the Abrahamic and the Mosaic. The Abrahamic covenant created the nation of Israel with Abraham

as its father. The Mosaic covenant established
the Law that would govern Israel. It is this second covenant that has been replaced by the new
covenant in Christ:

> *For if that first covenant had been fault-*
> *less, then should no place have been*
> *sought for the second.*
>
> *For finding fault with them, he saith, Be-*
> *hold, the days come, saith the Lord, when*
> *I will make a new covenant with the house*
> *of Israel and with the house of Judah:*
>
> *Not according to the covenant that I made*
> *with their fathers in the day when I took*
> *them by the hand to lead them out of the*
> *land of Egypt; because they continued not*
> *in my covenant, and I regarded them not,*
> *saith the Lord. (Hebrews 8:7-9)*

God's covenant with Abraham still stands and
is active even today. In the first appendix of this
publication is an article by Dr. Thomas McCall,
our staff theologian, which details God's present
covenantal relationship with the nation of Israel.
Israel also has a specific role to fulfill in End
Times prophecy. I would refer you to other materials available through Zola Levitt Ministries
that deal with prophecy and End Times events.

Many sincere Christians have been influenced

by replacement theology, which leads to a twisted understanding of Scripture. In another appendix, I have included a series of responses to a pastor's letter dealing with a request by a member of his congregation to attend a Passover seder. In his rebuke to this church member, the pastor demonstrates many of the errors that result from replacement theology. If God is indeed through with Israel, then Jewish traditions are obsolete and have no meaning, the Old Testament has no real value, and even Jews are no longer Jews. This line of reasoning doesn't fit with 2 Timothy 3:16-17, which states:

> *All Scripture is given by inspiration of God and is profitable for doctrine, for reproof, for correction, for instruction in righteousness: That the man of God may be perfect, throughly furnished unto all good works.*

When Paul wrote this, the New Testament had not yet been compiled, so the Scripture he was referring to was the Old Testament. God revealed Himself through those Scriptures for centuries in His dealings with Israel. God is the same, now and forever ("For I am the Lord, I change not. — Malachi 3:6). To say that the Old Testament is obsolete implies that we can learn nothing from it, as if the God of Israel is not the same God we serve today. Our access to God has changed (through Christ rather than a high priest), but God Himself will never change.

Note the pastor's answer to the question of "who is a real Jew." He states that when a Jew turns to Christ "he becomes like all other Gentiles, he becomes a Christian believer. There are not two classes of believers in the New Testament." He has confused our spiritual relationship with God through Christ and God's covenantal relationship to Israel established through Abraham. As Christians, we are saved by grace alone, through faith, and stand in a right relationship with God because of Christ's sacrifice on the cross. As the pastor correctly states, there are not two classes of believers in God's sight. However, a Jew who turns to Christ does not become "like all other Gentiles," because God's covenant with Abraham still stands. And as a physical descendant of Abraham, the Christian Jew shares in that covenant. That is why many Messianic Jews refer to themselves as "completed Jews." Through the Abrahamic covenant, God established a special people to demonstrate Himself to mankind, a nation through which He would bring a Savior who would redeem the world. A Messianic Jew can appreciate his special heritage, seeing in Christ the redemption promised long ago through Abraham.

God still has plans for the people of Israel. There is a remnant faithful to God. There are Messianic congregations everywhere, and they believe the same Christian doctrine as any other congregation. The present national unbelief of Israel was foreseen. It is a matter of prophecy that Israel would be in unbelief; that should not surprise us. As a matter of fact, it opened up an opportunity for the Gentiles. Because of Israel's falling away, there was room for the Gentiles to come in. Israel is judicially broken off from the good olive tree called Christ, but they are to be grafted in again. Paul points out:

> *And they* [Israel] *also, if they abide not still in unbelief, shall be grafted in: for God is able to graft them in again. For if thou wert cut out of the olive tree which is wild by nature, and were grafted contrary to nature into a good olive tree: how much more shall these* [Israel]*, which be the natural branches, be grafted into their own olive tree? (Romans 11:23-24)*

The replacement theologians seem to believe that Gentile Christians were not just grafted in, but that the entire olive tree was uprooted and replaced!

Paul also teaches very simply in Romans 15 that if you have profited by the spiritual things of Israel, then support Israel in worldly things (Rom. 15:27). You can do that by talking to replacement theologians, showing them from the Scripture what their error is and admonishing them not to curse Israel. God said, "I will bless them that bless thee, and I will curse them that curse thee." We would be well advised to take that to heart.

The Rabin Assassination
and Recent Terrorism

The assassination of Israeli Prime Minister Yitzhak Rabin provides a tragic example of misunderstandings on all sides caused at least in part by a lack of Bible knowledge. Those without an appreciation for biblical imperatives concerning Israel — not merely land grants but the sublime importance to God of Jewish possession of the Land — devalue territory in Israel. They will trade it for promises of peace from those long sworn to destroy the Jewish land and its people.

Whether or not peace comes, Scripture gives Israel not merely the West Bank but ultimately large portions of Jordan and Syria, and even Gaza and Egypt. (See Gen. 15:18) At press time, the Rabin assassination is still a recent occurrence and is difficult to interpret. The material which follows is taken from a letter sent in December 1995 to the subscribers of the author's ministry. It makes the point that the media everywhere, the Jews in America and Israel, and even the Palestinians are unable to interpret what really happened because of a lack of scriptural knowledge.

Israel's first assassination is being widely misunderstood. Supposedly, those who want peace supported Prime Minister Rabin, and those who are opposed to peace criticized him. Or so we are told. And finally "the opponents of peace" escalated their protests until one of them finally killed the Prime Minister. And now it's simply a question of whether Israel will follow Rabin's policies to perfect peace or fall into his opponents' clutches and continuous war.

That is the construction of the US media of a very complex and tragic event in Israel. Biblical people know better what's going on. In reality, this "peace process" has a terrible flaw. It violates a biblical imperative: the sanctity of the borders of Israel. In their time, Babylon, Persia, Greece and Rome, all mighty empires, changed the borders of Israel as they pleased. All of them are extinct. Israel is not an ordinary nation to be changed and manipulated according to the fortunes of men. It is God's land, and "God is not mocked" (Gal. 6:7).

Those who would seek political gain by this assassination are pointing out that the opposition in its protests called Rabin a traitor, and they say the invective is what killed him. But Israel is a democracy and necessarily has a divided government, as is ours in Washington, D.C. One part promotes a program and the other protests, and that is how it works both here and in

Israel. As to the "invective," a cartoon in the *Jerusalem Post* the day before Yom Kippur showed Rabin in full worship dress making his Day of Atonement confessions for the things he had called his opponents. Listed were "pariahs, parasites, crybabies, cancers, cowards, liars, idiots" and the list went on. Israeli politics have always contained such invective, and it's not strange to other democracies either. The fact is, the Prime Minister was shot by an overzealous Israeli crusading to maintain the biblical borders of Israel, and it's difficult for biblical people to condemn that goal.

One writer in the *Jerusalem Post* does not use the term "peace process," but calls it "the government's unilateral giveaway program." The "ultra extremist group," of American media expression, actually represents a probable majority of Israelis. "The opponents of peace" are simply those who object to giving half of their arable land to their sworn enemies and then hoping they are not annihilated. So far as the current clash goes, one could just as easily say the government started it with its extraordinary program of giving up the precious land of Israel for what has proved to be no peace at all.

We conducted a man-on-the-street

program for our upcoming *Jerusalem 3000* series, and I personally interviewed about fifteen people in downtown Jerusalem. Twelve or thirteen of them expressed extreme misgivings about the land for peace idea. Americans should realize that the "West Bank" describes biblical Judea and Samaria, and is a huge portion of Israel, not just a riverbank. The King of Jordan coined the expression "West Bank" to make the area seem small and unimportant, but it is the heart and soul of the Holy Land, and one glance at a map will show that. Many people I talked to felt it was a mistake to give up land of such proportions to people like the PLO. David Bar-Illan, the editor-in-chief of the *Jerusalem Post*, said in our October interview that Rabin was simply mistaken in his policies. When I pointed out that Rabin had fielded great armies against these very people and ought to know what he's doing, Bar-Illan said that great generals can make great mistakes.

Despite its incredible giveaway program, the government has never conducted a real referendum, a vote by all of the people, to understand if they support its policies. One Rabin government official said the huge number of people coming out to the funeral *is* the referendum, but he was not right. Policy by a democratic government must be with the consent of the governed, and the present Israeli government has never obtained that consent. The enemies of Israel include virtually all Arabs and all anti-Semites in the world, and that's quite a number of people! (It is not usually stated that there are 200 million Arabs and only 4 million Israelis. Our media maintains the myth that the Arabs are somehow the underdog.) Looking at the Arabs, one finds the real "opponents of peace." Hamas opposes any peace agreement with Israel, and its charter says as much: "The Hamas is opposed to all international conferences and negotiations and to any peaceful settlements." There were Arab celebrations in Lebanon and among the Hamas over the death of a man who even the dictators of Jordan and Egypt came to appreciate for his steadfastness and his character. While the world hastens to establish a 23rd Arab dictatorship in Israel, the Israeli "right wing" (as it is called by the American media) struggles to hold a very small land together. As to the PLO and Arafat, the Chairman did not attend the funeral because "he didn't want to be a distraction," as he said on the first day. On the second day, prompted by some PR man one could clearly hear on TV, he stated that he wanted to say goodbye to his friend, but "they [the Israelis] didn't give me this chance." In reality, Arafat did not attend the funeral because there is no peace and he would not have been welcome.

I am almost sorry to have to write this strong a letter after so sad an event, but the American media is so ridiculously misinformed, or so partisan toward a certain point of view, that it's hard to get any true picture of what's going on. CNN asked, "Can a nation that has seen so much bloodshed. . . ." Well, I've counted 27 days of war in Israel since 1948, as opposed to our own country's eight years in Vietnam and three years in Korea. Israel has lost some 3,000 soldiers, while we have lost 100,000. And we weren't fighting about our own country, in any case. Ted Koppel solemnly intoned, "A vision of Israelis killing Israelis — of what their country may become" in answer to the first case anyone can remember of an Israeli killing an Israeli. The ABC affiliate in Dallas said that the anti-government groups pose the greatest threat to security, when actually giving away the land to a sworn enemy obviously poses a still greater threat. Israel is unfortunately becoming to the news media and America what Jackie Kennedy was to the tabloids — a constant source of delicious drama and controversy. And yet we are talking here about God's country. Mike Wallace of *60 Minutes,* a reliable critic of Israel, had Kahane Chai members as interviewees, as if this tiny fringe group counted for something. To put such people on *60 Minutes* as representatives of Israel is to put Ku Klux Klan or neo-Nazis on television as representatives of America, and Wallace well knows it. About the only heartening American response to this terrible assassination was the presence of more than 100 Washington dignitaries at the funeral. Prime Minister Rabin had a warm personal relationship with a great many in the American government, and as a government we favor his party in Israeli politics.

So to wrap up all that I have said, Prime Minister Rabin was a fine Israeli gentleman, a distinguished soldier and a crusader for peace. His policies were extremely controversial and led in the end to his untimely death. Time will tell which side is right or wrong in this conflict — or the biblical End Times will come on and show that there really was no solution to the Israeli dilemma.

The tragedy of Rabin's death has been compounded by the continued murder of innocent people by the enemies of Israel. Israeli leaders have believed that giving away their land would buy them peace, but in February and March 1996 there was a spate of bombings that claimed over 50 lives. This ministry sent the following response to its readers in an April 1996 letter:

> This is a time to pray for the peace of Jerusalem, and Tel Aviv as well. Arafat's lack of control, the bomb makers of Gaza's Islamic University, and roving gangs of Palestinian terrorists have really done it this time. The rash of terrorism should surprise no *Levitt Letter* reader.
>
> As to the casualties, nothing much has been said other than to blame the victims, the Israelis. Hamas, the Palestinian gang supposed to have perpetrated these particular bombings, has said that the Israelis precipitated it by killing "the Engineer," the Hamas bomber who had claimed scores of innocent victims in bus bombings over a long period of time. Adding to that sort of reasoning was Walter Rodgers, CNN Israel bureau chief, with

his comment about terrorism in general: "Israel hasn't found a way to escape it." So apparently, for Hamas, Israel is supposed to keep quiet and let bombers finish off their civilians willy-nilly in public buses and not retaliate. And for Mr. Rodgers and CNN, it's up to the Israelis to twist and turn and figure out a way to stop being blown up. Silly Israelis, they just keep getting blown to pieces because they haven't "found a way to escape it."

CNN followed up two days after the Jerusalem bombing with a human interest story taped in a Palestinian home about two Palestinian men who happened to be driving a car past the ill-fated bus and were injured in the blast. Weeping women were pictured and sage men who gritted their teeth and muttered combative things about the Israelis. One young man made the point clearly that the death of Ayash, the so-called "Engineer," was the cause of it all. He concluded by saying that the one Palestinian killed died for God's purposes.

Ayash was not exactly a serial killer and not exactly a mass murderer. In truth, Ayash was one of the few serial mass murderers. This one man alone accounted for hundreds of casualties, scores of funerals, and was, of course, a first-rate criminal. We wonder if the shoe were on

the other foot, and if the Israelis ever re-
sorted to terrorism, how the Palestinians
would treat a character like Ayash.

The U.S. is suddenly sending help to
Israel to combat terrorism: some kind of
bomb-detecting devices and intelligence
information, plus American anti-terrorism
experts (from the folks who brought you
the World Trade Center and the Oklahoma
City bombings). Frankly, Israel would
have been better off if the U.S. had not
purchased a phony peace process in the
first place. The answer to Israel's problems is simply to go back all the way to
the day of the White House handshake and
"just say no." It shouldn't come as hot
news, but it's not wise to give away half
your territory to an enemy who swears to
destroy you.

Let me make a few points that may
not have quite hit the media. First of all,
there are not two kinds of Palestinians in
this world. The news would have it that
the vast majority are peace-loving Palestinians, and it's only those in a tiny group
called Hamas that don't want peace. In
reality, what all Palestinians want is the
land of Israel, peace or war. They want
the people of Israel thrown out of the
Middle East because they are a constant
humiliation to the 22 backward Arab

states that can't seem to make it into the twentieth century. The Israelis have built a modern democracy in one generation with some of the worst land in the whole area, and that galls the larger and richer dictatorships that surround them.

Second, this battle is not between the Palestinians and the Israelis, but between fundamentalist Islam and democracy. Israel is only the first of many targets in the Western world selected by Iran, Libya, Syria and the other rogue Arab states. The Moslem terrorists in Israel are funded from Iran, probably through Syrian auspices, and their mission is a small battle in a big war to be fought the world over in the twenty-first century. Presumably, the Moslem republics freed from the Soviet Union will join with Iran and the Middle Eastern Moslem powers to create quite a force to oppose the Western world. There are more Moslems in China than there are ethnic Chinese, and that's quite a number. Add those in as well, and you have a global conflict that could return the world to the Dark Ages if the Moslems prevail.

On the other hand, Bible people recognize that we are in an age when men cry, "Peace and safety," and we know what happens next: "sudden destruction cometh upon them" (I Thes. 5:3). All around us, men cry, "Peace, peace, when there is no peace" (Jer. 6:14), and it is all deeply suggestive of the end of the age. Amen; come, Lord Jesus.

The present leadership in Israel offers a wonderful working example of what happens when one does not comprehend the Scriptures. The books of Kings and Chronicles in the Bible are replete with rulers of Israel who were not conversant with the Word of God and led their people in strange directions. Two such rulers seem to be former Prime Minister Rabin and present Prime Minister Peres, "kings" of Israel, mistaking the most basic principle of Scripture, the land grant for the Jewish people.

In a *New York Times* article dated November 13, 1995, acting Israeli Prime Minister Peres, at a gathering in the newly renamed Yitzhak Rabin Square marking the end of shiva (the week of mourning for Rabin), described the mentality of those who oppose the peace process as being ". . . on the edge of insanity, who think they are God's messengers. In fact, they are the devil's disciples." *The Times* goes on to describe these people as defending ". . . what they hold to be biblical Jewish land." Certainly Scripture certifies the West Bank as Jewish land, along with the rest of Israel (see Ezek. 36).

For lack of knowledge of the Jewish Bible, the Jewish people will lose a large portion of the Land of Israel, and they will be the target of the whole world in the coming Tribulation, according to prophecy. They will unwittingly sign a peace covenant with a personality who will eventually turn on them, the Antichrist. And they will suffer enormous casualties in that mad, final battle of global warfare known as Armageddon. That all of these things concern Israel and that all are crystal clear in Scripture is not debatable. That the Jewish people, the authors of these very texts, have not read them or understood them is unconscionable.

As Scripture says, "My people are destroyed for lack of knowledge." (Hosea 4:6)

ENDNOTES

Unless otherwise noted, all scriptural quotations in this book are from the King James Version.

[1] Rev. C.I. Scofield, D.D., editor. *The Scofield Reference Bible*. Westwood, NJ: Barbour and Company, Inc., 1986.

[2] This booklet is discussed in more detail on pages 53-58 of the author's book *The Cairo Connection*.

[3] Merrill F. Unger with Zola Levitt. *God is Waiting to Meet You*. Chicago: Moody Press, 1975, pages 111-114.

[4] Zola Levitt. *The Miracle of Passover*. Zola Levitt Ministries, 1977, pages 11-12, 21-23.

[5] Anne Wilson Schaef. *Escape from Intimacy*. New York: HarperCollins Publishers, 1989, page 39.

[6] What the Dead Sea Scrolls give us is corroboration of the New Testament, not additional knowledge. They contain Scripture and obvious references to Jesus, or at least to a Messianic figure who was slain with piercings or wounds at exactly the time of Jesus and who is identified with the Messianic prophecy of Isaiah 11 and 53.

[7] Zola Levitt. *The Bible; The Whole Story*. Zola Levitt Ministries, 1983, page IV-9.

[8] J.B. Phillips. *Your God is Too Small*. New York: Macmillan Publishing Company, 1961, pages 26-27, 33, 52.

[9] *The Scofield Reference Bible*.

[10] Thomas McCall and Zola Levitt. *Once Through the New Testament*. Christian Herald, 1981, pages 138-143.

[11] *Works of John Wesley, Volume 1: Journal from October 14, 1735 to November 29, 1745.* Grand Rapids, MI: Zondervan Publishing House, reprint of the 1872 edition, pages 98-103.

[12] For more information on the Dead Sea Scrolls, I would refer you to our *Secrets of the Scrolls* videos and transcript, which are available through our ministry.

[13] Although Scripture does indicate, in the "wheat and tares" passage of Matthew 13:25-30 and other places, that until the Lord's return there will be unbelievers in the church.

[14] *The Bible; The Whole Story*, pages V-1 to V-11.

[15] Many people believe that Luke was a Gentile, but this belief appears to be based on tradition rather than biblical evidence. Most often cited is his profession as a physician and his Gentile name. However, there is no reason to suppose that there were no Jewish physicians at the time of Christ, and other prominent Jews went by Gentile names (most notably Peter and Paul). Although Luke's background is not given, evidence for his Jewishness can be found in his intimate knowledge of Temple practices (such as in his account of Zacharias in Luke 1) and his close acquaintance with Mary (who evidently revealed to him those things she had hidden in her heart which are cited in Luke 2). It is also significant that in Acts 21 when Paul was accused of bringing a Gentile into the Temple, it was Trophimus rather than Luke who was mentioned by the accusers.

I would like to acknowledge Dr. Thomas S. McCall for his excellent suggestions and Beth Mull for her editing work, as well as the Christians and the Jews whose friendship and tolerance I have so deeply valued.

A current list of Zola Levitt's books, cassettes, albums, videos, and other materials is available at no charge from:

ZOLA
P. O. Box 12268
Dallas, TX 75225-0268